Memoirs *and* MISCELLANEOUS Ramblings

EDGAR RUSSELL, JR.

Memoirs and MISCELLANEOUS Ramblings

Copyright ©2018 by Edgar Russell, Jr.

All rights reserved. No part of this book may be reproduced, copied, stored or transmitted in any form or by any means – graphic, electronic, or mechanical, including photocopying, recording, or information storage and retrieval systems without the prior written permission of Edgar Russell, Jr. or HOV Publishing except where permitted by law.

HOV Publishing a division of HOV, LLC.
www.hovpub.com
hopeofvision@gmail.com

Cover Design: HOV Design Solutions
Editor: Bettye Walker

Write the Author Edgar Russell, Jr. at:
fixrus1@yahoo.com

For more information about special discounts for bulk purchases, please visit www.hovpub.com

ISBN 978-1-942871-45-3
Library of Congress Control Number: 2018962099

10 9 8 7 6 5 4 3 2 1

Printed in the United States of America

DEDICATION

This book is dedicated to La Verne, my wife of almost 59 years and mother of our five now adult children -- Faith, Bridgette, Lisa, Edgar and John – in memory of her selfless love and boundless devotion to her family.

ACKNOWLEDGEMENTS

In recognition of the indelible influence on my life of George and Edna Miller, a childless couple of no relation, who provided shelter in their home for me, my siblings and our mother following the breakup of her marriage with Dad. They gave us needed stability along with a healthy mix of love, guidance and discipline.

TABLE OF CONTENTS

Introduction 1

PART 1: MEMOIRS 6
  My Earliest Memories 7
  Living with Grandpa 10
  The Millers 14
  Mom Comes to the Millers 16
  Living with the Millers 19
  College and Uncle Sam 23
  Ms. Holley and Ms. Woody 27
  Life in the Military 29
  Ed and La Verne Meet 34
  Proposal and Marriage 40
  La Verne and Mom 52
  Fatherhood 55
  Thoughts on La Verne 58
  Mom as a Mother 65
  Dad as a Father 68
  Family Tree of Siblings 71
  Siblings 72
  La Verne's Poem 75
  Instinct 76

PART 2: MISCELLANEOUS RAMBLINGS 78
Mr. Miller: "A Child of Slavery and a Hero" 79
She Is With Me 84
A Memorable Drive 85
A Memorable Outing 88
A Pistol Packing Christmas 92
The Search for Freedom 95
A New Paradise 99
Back Yards 105
Believe or Not 106
Blame It On Aladdin 111
Can Gerbils Do Arithmetic? 114
Caribbean Odyssey 118
Charles Russell: "A True Friend" 122
Chilly Grandma 127
Coming Soon: "A New Holiday" 129
Conflicted 130
The Joy of Competition—The Agony of Defeat 135
Dinner for Two 137
Doing the Right Thing 139
Don't Call Me Polly 143
Down with Akrasia 146
Family Matters Matter 149
Freedom 152

Green 154

Henry Jeffries 155

How Much Can One Friend Bear? 160

Seeing Is Not Always Believing 165

Lost 167

Nick Names and Pain 171

Patriotism 173

Presumptions Can Lead to Assumptions 175

Reunion 181

Sam Adams, Jr. 184

Echo the Houseguest 187

The Matador and The Bull 188

Confessions of an Unusual Dog 192

The Vote 196

To Believe or Not Believe 198

The Seasons 199

PART 3: REFLECTIONS 201

ABOUT THE AUTHOR

Edgar Russell, Jr. started thinking about the world of communications from the time he was a teenager. From the moment he saw his first feature film, showing news reporters as defenders of the public—in their daily enterprise of fighting corruption and exposing wrong doing in places high and low—he was hooked. His early aspirations were further enhanced by his avid reading of black-owned newspapers like the Pittsburgh Courier, Chicago Defender and Baltimore Afro-American, who dispatched news reporters around the country. The focus of their mission was always devoted to the singular cause of exposing this nation's racial, social and economic ills in an effort to achieve a more just society for all citizens.

Aside from his brief stint as a Radio News Announcer, shortly after graduating from college as a Journalism major, Edgar never realized his dream of becoming a crusading news reporter. He did, however, enjoy a rewarding and fulfilling 40-year career in Communications, working for the government, corporate and non-profit sectors. During this forty-year period, he spent seven of those years reporting and writing for the U.S. Information Agency. This included reporting on the United Nations General Assembly sessions, Justice Department, Civil

Rights Movement, "Freedom Rides" of the sixties and/or any laws mandating racially segregated seating on interstate travel.

Prior to his retirement after 23 years of service at IBM, Edgar held various professional and management assignments including employee communications and education programs, advertising, promotion and sales, as well as press relations on IBM's involvement in NASA space exploration initiatives.

Following his retirement from IBM, he invested another 10 years with the United Ways of Greater New Haven and Milford, Connecticut, working in the areas of Marketing and Communications. Afterwards, he spent another 10 years serving as a substitute teacher in the New Haven, Hamden and Cheshire, Connecticut Public High Schools.

Edgar currently resides in Milford, Connecticut. Active in two creative writing groups at the Milford Senior Center, Edgar occasionally exercises his zest for writing by periodic contributions to the "Letter to the Editor" section of local newspapers.

Widowed since 2013 (and defined by his own terminology as an 88-year-old "senior" senior citizen), Edgar considers himself to be a man of faith and a Believer who finds special joy in fellowshipping with members of Milford's First Baptist Church. One of his other favorite and top joys is frequently engaging in discourse on sundry topics with his adult children, grandchildren and members of his extended family.

Introduction

At the writing of this memoir I am 84 years old and have lost my wonderful wife and life partner of nearly 59 years, La Verne, on October 11, 2013. After my wife's passing, it seemed appropriate (even therapeutic) for me to chronicle some of the steps that got me from where I was back then to where I am now, to pass these life experiences onto my adult children and grandchildren.

This by no means is meant to be a definitive and complete history of my life. I simply wanted to highlight some of the more meaningful experiences and precious moments of life as I recollect them. As a matter of record, I have included a chronology of my education and work experience, following this brief Introduction.

I consider myself fortunate in that I have had a very successful and varied career since graduating from college in 1956. In hindsight, I must say that each assignment has proven to be an invaluable experience in learning. My initial goal upon entering college was to become a news reporter for a major newspaper. Although I did realize my ultimate goal after graduating from Duquesne University, I was fortunate to have worked as a News Announcer for Radio Station WILY and as an Advertising Copy Writer for the

Pittsburgh Courier, before securing employment in the federal government as a Writer and Reporter for the United States Information Agency (USIA).

While at USIA, I provided coverage for a number of federal agencies, the United Nations General Assembly Sessions and many of the important civil rights protests occurring during that time. In 1965, I was granted the opportunity to work for IBM, providing communications support for many of the NASA spaceflight programs; including Mercury, Gemini, Apollo-Saturn, the Space Shuttle and a number of "unmanned" space missions. The highlight of my career, however, was my coverage of "manned" space missions and United Nations assignments.

After retiring from IBM in 1988, I decided to do absolutely nothing for about two years. La Verne and I took our first ocean voyage and a coast-to-coast railroad trip from New York to California. In 1990, I joined the United Way, working as Marketing Director for the United Way of New Haven and Milford, Connecticut. After retiring from United Way in 1997, my daughter Bridgette suggested that I explore opportunities as a substitute teacher in Connecticut's Public School System. I subsequently worked as a Substitute Teacher for the school districts of New Haven, Hamden, Cheshire and Trumbull for the next 12 years. In 2011, at the age of 81, I stopped teaching and from that time until now have remained unemployed and fully retired.

I am blessed to have had a lot of variety and fulfillment in my various occupations. I am equally blessed to have had such a loving and caring wife, as well as loving and supportive children and grandchildren. My cup runs over with thanksgiving in my heart. And in honor of those that I love, I leave this legacy of my life.

Edgar Russell, Jr., Author

EDGAR RUSSELL, JR.

Life Events

Birth:	January 13, 1930 | Pittsburgh, PA
Marriage:	La Verne Millicent Rucks December 31, 1954 | Pittsburgh, PA
Children:	Faith, Bridgette, Lisa, Edgar III, John

Education & Work Experience

1935 – 1947 Bluestone Public High School \| Bramwell, WV
Diploma

1947 – 1948 Bluefield State College \| Bluefield, WV
Non-Matriculated (Left after one year to join the military)

1948 – 1952 United States Air Force \| Airman First Class
Tours of Duty:
Okinawa and Newfoundland
Honorable Discharge

1952 – 1956 Duquesne University \| Pittsburgh, PA
B.A., Journalism

1956 – 1957 Radio Station WILY \| Pittsburgh, PA

	Radio News Announcer / Advertising Copy Writer
1958	Pittsburgh Courier | Pittsburgh, PA *Advertising Copy Writer*
1958 – 1965	U.S. Information Agency (USIA) | Washington, DC *Writer & Reporter*
1965 – 1988	IBM | Multiple Locations *Writer & Communications Manager*
1990 – 1995	United Way of Greater New Haven | New Haven, CT *Marketing Director*
1995 – 1997	United Way of Milford | Milford, CT *Marketing Director*
1998 – 2003	New Haven Public Schools | New Haven, CT *Substitute Teacher*
2004 – 2005	Hamden Public Schools | Hamden, CT *Substitute Teacher*
2006 – 2009	Cheshire Public Schools | Cheshire, CT *Substitute Teacher*
2009 – 2010	Trumbull School System | Trumbull, CT *Substitute Teacher*

PART 1:
MEMOIRS

PART 1: MEMOIRS

My Earliest Memories

My earliest memories of mom and dad were around the age of two. I recall us living in an apartment on the second floor, in a building owned by the Bramwell Masonic Lodge in Bramwell, West Virginia. It was the place where my parents settled after returning from Pittsburgh, PA.

Following their marriage in March 1929 (mom was only 16 and dad was 23), they decided to move to Pittsburgh to find work in the steel mills and live with dad's older sister, Mable. For some odd reason never fully explained to me, the job search did not go as planned and they were forced to move back to Bramwell. I was about six months old when they returned.

Born January 13, 1930 in Pittsburgh—the first of five children. The place where I was born held a certain distinction when I started the public school for colored students in 1935. Being the only kid in my class not born in West Virginia, I became the brunt of classroom jokes. Unable to pronounce the word Pittsburgh correctly, my classmates frequently substituted a "s" for the "t's" which ended up sounding more like Pissburg than Pittsburgh.

A year later in 1931, my sister Ida was born; followed by my brother Roland in 1934, my sister Doris in

PART 1: MEMOIRS

1935 and my sister Odessia in 1939. Our family continued to live in the apartment owned by the Masonic Lodge for about nine years. I vividly remember the ups and downs of my parents' relationship quite well. Some of those memories included the good times had by all when we picnicked outside on the backside of our apartment.

Dad would build a fire in a cleared area of the yard and we would use wire hangers for a "wiener roast." We would put a frankfurter (hot dog) on the pointed end of a hangar and hold the hangar over the fire until it was brown and roasted. Mom sang in the Bluestone Baptist Church Choir back then; and on Sundays she would often go to church, leaving my dad to complete the family dinner.

As I recall, the major issue between my mom and dad before they separated had to do with him not finding steady work. Mom occasionally worked as a cook and maid for some of the affluent families in town. Personally, I do not think dad was lazy because he was well-respected by the families he did projects for. He simply did not make enough money to support a family of our size. When our family became financially strained, the Millers (George and Edna) would chip in to help.

The Millers were a childless couple of no family relation, who had brought my mother (an orphaned teenage)

PART 1: MEMOIRS

from Virginia to live with them in their home and to attend the Bramwell Public School for Colored Students. After mom met and married dad, the apartment they settled in was directly across the railroad side of a creek that divided the town—a "hollering distance" from where the Millers lived.

Sometimes we went over to their house to eat. At other times, Edna (who insisted on being called by her first name) would bring something over to our apartment to eat. While I was aware of the ongoing arguments between mom and dad, I never thought the day would come when those arguments would result in the split of our family. Roland and I eventually moved in with our dad and grandfather while Ida, Doris, Odessia and my mom moved in with the Miller's.

PART 1: MEMOIRS

Living with Grandpa

People often say that life has its ups and downs. I cannot think of even one "upside" to living with my grandpa. When my dad brought Roland and I to live with grandpa, he was living in a tiny apartment atop a garage, off an unpaved street called "the alley." He was sickly and feeble, saddled with a number of physical problems including alcohol addiction and extremely bitter about his circumstances.

Grandpa formerly worked for one of the wealthiest families in the town of Bramwell as a groundskeeper, groomsman, driver and overall handyman. Based on the standards of pay in that day, he made a decent amount of money. He and grandma had raised four daughters and a son. Mr. Freeman, his employer had promised him a life-long pension and the ownership of the place where he resided. However, after old Mr. Freeman died, his heirs decided to do otherwise, reducing grandpa's overall pension and charging him a monthly fee for residing in the apartment. This forced him to apply for "relief" under the social services program of West Virginia.

By now, grandma had been dead for nearly five years. Grandpa was barely subsisting on his own when dad, my brother and I came to live with him. I can only imagine,

PART 1: MEMOIRS

if I were faced with such circumstances I would probably be bitter too. After a couple of months my dad took off for Pittsburgh—in his constant search for meaningful employment—leaving Roland and me with our grandpa.

There were no decent paying jobs for unskilled laborers in Southern West Virginia other than the coal mines, which my dad had always shunned. So, out of desperation he sought employment once again in the city, known at the time as the steel producing capital of the world. After dad left, Roland and I would occasionally go to Mr. Miller and Edna's place to visit with our mom and sisters.

Grandpa had a brother who lived about 30 miles outside of Bramwell. When his brother died, his wife (Aunt Ellen) came to live with us; and an already unpleasant situation became even worse. The one positive thing I remember about Aunt Ellen is she was great at walking us to the homes of some of the families in town, so we could get a hot meal.

One of Aunt Ellen's friends had a bad habit of chewing a tobacco-like substance called snuff. The juice from her chewing the snuff would occasionally form at the ends of her mouth. One day, while waiting for her to fix us a plate of food, my brother informed me that he saw some of the juice from the snuff fall into the food. We promptly let

PART 1: MEMOIRS

Aunt Ellen know that we were not eating any of this woman's food, despite the fact that there was nothing to eat back home. Aunt Ellen insisted that we eat the food anyway and so we did.

There was also the time when Roland was too sick to go to school. I remember Aunt Ellen preparing a homemade concoction to rid Roland of what she called "the poison" in his body. The second day, Roland still was not feeling well and was increasingly running a high fever. Aunt Ellen suggested that I go over to Mr. Miller and Edna's place to inform my mother. Mom came quickly, contacting the town doctor who diagnosed Roland with diphtheria, a type of bacterial infection.

It took several days of treatment before Roland was well enough to return to school. I remember mom being a bit annoyed with Aunt Ellen and grandpa for not contacting her sooner. She was convinced that neither of them had given Roland the proper attention he needed. Mom promised to bring all of us together soon.

True to her word, it was not long before Roland and I found ourselves at the Miller's reunited with our mother and sisters, with the six of us sharing one bedroom. Mom used a curtain to section off the room, diving two-thirds of the room for her and my sisters; and leaving one-third of the

PART 1: MEMOIRS

space for me and Roland to share a cot that we both slept in. My brother slept at the foot of the cot while I slept at the head. This was our usual day-to-day accommodations until Edna purchased a pullout couch for the living room. At night, the couch was converted into a bed for me to sleep in while Roland continued to enjoy the comforts of the cot all to himself. We both were very happy. Mr. Miller and Edna, having no children of their own, now found their comfortable two-bedroom bungalow-style home, overflowing with five little Russell kids and their mother.

PART 1: MEMOIRS

The Millers

Edna was a very fair-skinned woman with long red hair and was known around Bramwell as the "whitest looking" Negro in town. She hailed from Martinsville, Virginia and was rumored to have not known who her father was. However, people speculated that her father was most assuredly White, given the complexion of her skin.

Edna's second marriage to Mr. Miller occurred during her early twenties. Mr. Miller was a very dark-skinned man of short stature with a big chest and muscular arms. A graduate of Lincoln University, in Philadelphia, PA., Mr. Miller was one of the few African Americans in town (outside of the school teachers) who had a college degree.

How Mr. Miller and Edna met each other, God only knows. But I was told that when they met, Edna was a widow and had lost her husband in a coal mining accident. To know Edna, and spend time around her, one would never guess that she lacked a formal education. Her schooling did not extend beyond the second or third grade, which meant that she never learned to read or write. Mr. Miller took it upon himself to teach Edna basic reading and writing skills; and out of sheer

PART 1: MEMOIRS

will and determination, Edna continued to educate herself until she became the savvy woman that we all knew.

Mr. Miller and Edna were a very interesting couple. They were about as opposite as two people could possibly be given their interests and personality. They never had any children of their own, but their home was always occupied with someone else's offspring. They had unofficially become "foster parents" to many children, eventually including my Mother and her brood.

Mr. Miller and Edna were staunch Baptists and very active charter members of the Bluestone Baptist Church. Edna was a missionary and member of the Board of Christian Education, as well as other diverse organizations. Mr. Miller oversaw the music ministry and served as the choir director and church trustee. (I do not recall him ever becoming a deacon).

The one golden rule among many that the Millers were insistent upon was that everyone residing in their household should attend Sunday school and church on Sunday's. Having a social life after church meant going to church first. So that is exactly what we did.

PART 1: MEMOIRS

Mom Comes to the Millers

When mom moved from Virginia to West Virginia to live with the Millers, both of her adoptive parents (Ida and John Murphy) were in failing health. From what I am told, mom really did not want to leave her adoptive parent's but they convinced her otherwise. Shortly after moving in with the Miller's, she was immediately enrolled into the Bluestone High School for "colored" students.

Mom was a country girl. Back home in the Chestnut Knob section of Martinsville, Virginia, she was known by all of her friends as "love." But this new environment posed a challenge for her in that the moment she arrived, she felt ill at ease and intimidated by her surroundings. While she had what everyone agreed was a pretty face and an agreeable disposition, her physique was rather big-boned in size for a girl her age. She would often describe herself as having been a gawky 13-year-old girl, who was forced to don the hand-me-downs and out-of-fashion clothes that Edna gave her to wear. Despite these setbacks, mom proved to be a very focused student. Although her study habits were on par, her social life and social interaction was a complete disaster.

When mom entered the ninth grade she met a young man named Edgar Russell, who would eventually become

PART 1: MEMOIRS

my father. A celebrated football star at Bluestone High School, dad was what you might describe as a "professional" student. He started playing football in the ninth grade. He continued playing the sport for seven years without ever graduating from high school. At the time, the rules for playing sports were obviously very lax, which proved a welcome convenience for the team since dad was their star ball carrier. If he were to graduate, then he obviously would not be able to play anymore. When dad met my mother, he had been in the twelfth grade for three consecutive years. She was 15 and he was 22 at the time. By the time they got married a year later, mom had not completed the 9th grade and dad never completed the 12th grade.

A somewhat comely, wiry built man, dad was by no means a handsome guy. However, due to his football prowess, he was renowned for being one of the more popular students at Bluestone. With a football in hand, few could catch or tackle him due to his speed and shiftiness (traits which were not substantially passed onto Roland or me despite the fact that we also played football in high school).

Dad and mom first met at a school dance following one of his games. How things transpired from that point on, I do not know. But what I do know is they married a year later when mom was 16 and dad was 23. Since there was no

PART 1: MEMOIRS

steady employment for an uneducated Black man in Bramwell (and since dad abhorred working in the coal mines), the young couple moved to Pittsburgh, Pennsylvania, where my dad's older sister, Mabel, lived with her husband, Cephas.

Uncle Cephas was a steel mill worker and extremely optimistic when it came to helping dad secure a steady job in the well-paying steel industry. Meanwhile, mom was pregnant with me, her firstborn child. As it turns out, things did not work out as Uncle Cephas had planned. Six months after my birth, mom found herself having come full circle: She had moved to Bramwell to live with the Millers, met and married dad, leaving Bramwell for a new life in Pittsburgh, only to return again to Bramwell, living in an apartment a stone's throw away from the Millers residence.

PART 1: MEMOIRS

Living with the Millers

Though food was occasionally scarce, there was always something to eat at the Millers and we never went to bed hungry. Both mom and Edna were quick to share whatever we were having for dinner with one of the boys we played with. Somehow, this boy always managed to be around when dinner was being served. Sometimes, Roland and I were not particularly happy when he came around because it meant that there was less for us to eat. Still, it taught us an important lesson: Always be willing to share.

While Edna and Mom worked as maids and cooks in the affluent homes of well-to-do White folks in town, Mr. Miller derived his income from a myriad of "mysterious" white-collar jobs—jobs which I assumed must have been legal since he had no known run-ins with the law. There was also the occasional letter from dad while living in Pittsburgh which occasionally contained a bit of cash. Although, more often than not, the letters we received from him were empty promises to send us money at some later date.

Mr. Miller became a father figure in our lives. He was very stern and did not brook any "sassiness" or talking back on our parts to adults. He and Edna were what we often described as "Abraham Lincoln Republicans," in that the

PART 1: MEMOIRS

only time the word Democrats would spill from their mouths was when it was preceded by a four-letter word beginning with a "d" and rhyming with ram.

There were a number of rigid rules to follow at the dinner table. Hands and arms were required to remain off the table at all times. There was no drinking of any form of liquid until our meal had been entirely consumed. And we were not allowed to speak or talk unless we were responding to a question posed by an adult. When Mr. Miller sat at the head of the table there was no deviation from the rules. But when he was absent, things were a bit more lax, which allowed for a more relaxing and enjoyable time.

As a father figure, Mr. Miller had a special infinity for me and my younger sister Odessia. All of my brothers and sisters were fairly good students but none of them received the academic focus from Mr. Miller that I did. Out of all my siblings, I was the one he thought would one-day go to college. He called Odessia his "little buddy" and she called him "Buddy." Odessia was the only person who could call him that. As for the rest of us, we had to call him Mr. Miller.

During my senior year of high school, I lived off and on with one of my dad's sisters, Willie Ann. Aunt Willie Ann was married to a coal miner and the two of them lived

PART 1: MEMOIRS

in a town not far from Bramwell. My mom started dating a man named Maceo Ramey and by the time I moved back home, Maceo had become somewhat of a fixture in the house.

Neither of the Millers were home very often. Mr. Miller was away managing a small restaurant he would later acquire. Edna traveled extensively, attending one church function or convention after another. None of my siblings liked the idea of having Maceo becoming their step dad. Personally, I could not wait to graduate so I could get away from it all. My younger siblings envied me for having the freedom to leave. They constantly teased me that I was the one who would eventually escape.

Prior to my graduation, Mr. Miller and I came to an understanding that I would move to Pittsburgh to stay with dad and seek employment for the summer. The expectation was that I would hopefully return home with most of my savings. In turn, Mr. Miller would help me financially to enroll in Bluefield State College in Bluefield, West Virginia.

Dad worked for a wall washing contractor, named Kirk Kirkpatrick, who allowed him to rent a room in his home at an affordable rate. When I arrived, Mr. Kirkpatrick hired me in his employ as well. For the next three months (June to August 1947), I worked and shared dad's room. Mr.

PART 1: MEMOIRS

Kirkpatrick's wife slowly became a second mother to me, insisting that I call her Elsie.

Once the summer was over, I returned home to Bluefield and was greeted with several surprises. Maceo and mom were married and had a child together. My sister, Ida, had graduated from high school and left home with a close friend to find employment in New York City. Roland had moved to upstate New York and was now living with dad's sisters, Jo Ann and Mary, both of which were employed at a canning factory in Oakfield, New York. The only remaining children left at home from the original five were Doris and Odessia. Although I loved my new brother James, I had an almost instant dislike for his father—the man who I personally felt did not treat my mother right.

Maceo, to my knowledge, had never been married or fathered any children of his own. He had acquired a job in the coal mines and was making good wages but he was also a man who loved to gamble. After the birth of James, two additional children—Ronney and Everette—followed in rapid succession. What was once a family of five had now expanded to family of eight. As the Ramey family grew, the Russell kids continued to leave the nest, either by way of graduation or marriage. Throughout the entire transition, Doris and Odessia were the only ones to remain in place.

PART 1: MEMOIRS

College and Uncle Sam

There were no scholarships available at the time for me to attend college and neither of my parents were in a position to help financially. Working in Pennsylvania for the summer had allowed me to accumulate a decent amount of savings. That, coupled with Mr. Miller's generosity and financial support, allowed me to enroll into Bluefield State College as an off-campus student in 1947.

Blanche, a close friend of my mothers who had grown up with mom in Martinsville and had similar ties to the Miller's, arranged for me to rent a room from a family in Bluefield for a modest price. To help with my living expenses, I secured a job as a dishwasher in Bluefield's only sea food restaurant. Academically, I did fairly well at Bluefield State during my freshman year, maintaining a B+ average. However, if I were to attend for a second year, then I would need to secure some funds to do so. Since Mr. Miller was not doing that well economically, I was resolved to returning to McKeesport, to seek employment and save as much money as I could for my second year of college.

I found a job in a local steel mill as a temporary employee, making good money—more than I had ever made before. Unfortunately, I did not have the discipline to save

PART 1: MEMOIRS

most of it. So, when the summer job had ended and it was time to reenroll into Bluefield State, I did not have sufficient funds to attend. Mr. Miller was extremely proud of my first-year success at Bluefield State. Somewhat embarrassed by my financial dilemma and not wanting to be of further burden on Mr. Miller who was in failing health, I decided to write a letter to him. In the letter, I advised him that I would not be returning to Bluefield State for a second term and instead was planning to enlist into the U.S. Air Force, with the intent of serving for three years. Afterwards, I would return to Bluefield State to resume my studies.

I enlisted in the U.S. Air Force in 1948. After basic training I returned home, promising Mr. Miller that I would save a portion of my military pay to complete my studies at Bluefield State. Mr. Miller always hoped for the best for me but, knowing him as I did, I was fairly certain he was not entirely convinced concerning my motives, since I had shown no real propensity for saving up to that point.

With the emergence of the Korean War came the *G.I. Bill of Rights* (also known as the *Servicemen's Readjustment Act*) with all its entitlements. The G.I. Bill was made available for all servicemen at that time and provided me with the means to finally complete my studies at Bluefield State. But sadly, Mr. Miller did not live long

PART 1: MEMOIRS

enough to see that day happen, passing away while I was still on active duty in Okinawa.

After my discharge from the Air Force in 1952 (after serving three years, eight months and five days), I returned home to West Virginia for a brief visit. A lot of changes had taken place in our family: Roland had enlisted in the Navy, where he served for some 20 plus years. Ida Mae was now living in Brooklyn, New York with her husband and daughter Debby. Doris and Odessia had gotten married, leaving Edna, my mother, Maceo and their three children as remaining tenants in the home.

Mom and Edna had assumed that I would resume my studies at Bluefield State for a second year. Instead, I decided to transfer to a college in Pennsylvania, with the hope of attending either the University of Pittsburgh or Duquesne University. My plan was to live off campus, commuting back and forth between school and a part-time job, supplemented my GI-bill financing. I reconnected with the Kirkpatrick family, who had previously provided me with a place to stay when I first moved to McKeesport with my dad.

My first choice for college enrollment was the University of Pittsburgh. I was enamored by the notion that one of their main buildings was called *The Cathedral of*

PART 1: MEMOIRS

Learning—a multi-story high rise that easily dominated the University of Pittsburgh landscape. When I prepared to enroll in September 1952, prospective students were herded together in long lines in the cavernous basement of the *Cathedral*. It reminded me of the military and lining up for inspection. Although I appreciated my military service, I did not need this reminder. As fate would have it, I found myself quickly getting out of the University of Pittsburgh, opting to enroll instead at the smaller quieter campus of Duquesne University. To this day, I have never regretted my decision.

PART 1: MEMOIRS

Ms. Holley and Ms. Woody

The two teachers who had the greatest impact on my life were my former high school instructors, Ms. Woody and Ms. Holley. Both were single and had never married. Both were stern taskmasters who made the most of the second-hand teaching materials they had at their disposal.

A Science Teacher by trade, Ms. Woody made the subject of science so intriguing that it peaked a person's curiosity about life. Our books and learning materials were often had hand-me-downs, comprised of torn texts, leaky test tubes and specimen handling equipment like clamps and forceps that no longer worked as originally designed. Nothing we had was ever new or in top condition, but Ms. Woody rarely complained or made excuses for it. She taught, and you learned. If you had trouble grasping a concept, she took the time to work with you one-to-one. A small petite woman, Ms. Woody always maintained complete control of her class. Would-be trouble makers soon learned not to mess with Ms. Woody.

Aside from her prowess as a Science Teacher, Ms. Woody was extremely proud of her racial heritage. Before the cries of Black pride and "Black is beautiful," that were echoed during the turbulent struggles of the 60's, Ms.

PART 1: MEMOIRS

Woody had us all believing in the innovative resilience of Black folks in the 40's, who knew how to take the hand me downs from White schools and do better with them than they had. It gave us a sense of pride about ourselves and we believed and lived out our school motto: *Bluestone boys and girls are always ladies and gentlemen.*

Ms. Holley was an English teacher who loved literature. When she spoke, her English was of such eloquence that it surpassed the skills of any person I knew, Black or White, who lived in West Virginia. It was through Ms. Holley that I fell in love with the English language and literature in written and spoken form. Ms. Holley was insistent that I practice enunciating and pronouncing my words correctly, so I could read and speak clearly and properly. Of course, she never hesitated to reprimand me for what she termed as "lazy speech." As a result of Ms. Holly, I became such a stickler for using correct pronunciation when I spoke that my classmates nicknamed me "Jug head." I never learned the rationale for the linkage.

While I still, no doubt, have a trace of West Virginia "twang" from time to time when speaking, I am careful to never speak flat or in a drawl in honor of Ms. Holley's sterling efforts on my behalf.

PART 1: MEMOIRS

Life in the Military

I was an 18-year-old boy coming into manhood when I enlisted in the U.S. Air Force. The date I officially enlisted was October 8, 1948 at the Armed Forces Recruitment Center in McKeesport, Pennsylvania. After a brief trip home to Bramwell, to say goodbye to my mom and siblings, I was on a train headed for Lackland Air Force Base in San Antonio, Texas for basic training.

My original term of service in the military was only for three years but, when the Korean War broke out in 1950, President Harry Truman froze all military discharges pending the outcome of the war. I would later serve an additional eight months and five days due to a military freeze—serving initially in Okinawa, Japan and later in Newfoundland. Some of my stateside assignments included posts at air force bases in Texas, Michigan, Colorado, New Jersey and California. I was honorably discharged from the Air Force on June 12, 1952 at the Westover Massachusetts Air Force Base.

I was 22-years-old, a young man wizened by his military experience and eager to get on with his life as a civilian. When I initially enlisted into military service, I entertained thoughts of applying for training as a pilot. I had

PART 1: MEMOIRS

read about the adventures of the *Tuskegee Airmen* and saw a lot of glamour in what they did. I initiated an application for pilot training shortly after completion of basic training. I renewed the application after arriving in Okinawa but never received a response. I finally resolved myself to the fact that my Air Force days would be spent largely on the ground, looking at the planes as they flew overhead, servicing them when they landed and performing other ancillary responsibilities.

    The disciplines of the military did not bother me. In fact, I turned out to be a pretty good airman. At the time of my discharge, I had risen through the ranks from an Airman to Airman First Class (three stripes), the equivalent of a Sergeant in the Army. The branches of service were pretty much segregated, especially when it came to basic training. Although both Black and White airmen were stationed at Lackland AFB, we had separate training facilities in different sectors of the base. The only time our units came together was for base parades. When I shipped out to serve in Japan, I was assigned to an all-Black Engineering Aviation Battalion based in Naha Okinawa.

    Two things stood out about my assignment in Naha, Okinawa: One, I was immediately made a mail clerk since the top sergeant noticed from my chart that I had been to

PART 1: MEMOIRS

college. Two, I quickly discovered that adjusting to service in Okinawa was not going to be easy. During the first week of my assignment I noticed a military ambulance unloading a casket onto a transport plane. I asked one of the airmen who had been in Okinawa for a while if he knew what had happened. He told me the deceased airman had gotten into a fight over a game of cards. Some "stir crazy" airman (the name given to someone who had been stationed in Okinawa for an extended period of time) hit him in the head with a plank and he never recovered. Thinking they must have been playing poker or black jack for money, I asked:

"What type of card game were they playing?"

"Bid whist," he replied.

At the time I did not know how to play bid whist, nor was I interested in learning. In my mind, any guy who gets killed over a card game with no money involved, did not make sense. Oddly enough, after being on Okinawa for about four months and becoming "stir crazy" from boredom, I found the game quite satisfying. Like most of my "stir crazy" buddies, I took the game very seriously—although not to the extent of getting hit in the head with a plank or being the one doing the hitting.

After several months of duty with my "all Black" outfit, I was called into the Captain's office and told that I was being reassigned to another unit. President Truman had just signed an order desegregating the U.S. military. I was a part of the vanguard and breakup of the original "all Black" *822nd Engineering Aviation Battalion*, with most of our members being reassigned and transferred to what were formerly "all White" units.

I was transferred to the *6303rd Air Terminal Squadron* in Kadena, Okinawa and assigned the task of supervising the loading of cargo on/off transport aircraft. The first thing I noticed, when I reported to my new assignment, was a line of guitars hanging on the walls of the barracks. I thought to myself: "Welcome home to the good old boy country." But, as it turned out, I never had an incident with any of my new colleagues, many of whom were from southern states within the United States.

When my tour in Okinawa was over I was transported by ship back to California. Our ship was the last to be allowed out of Okinawa during the early stages of the Korean War. A number of deteriorating battlefield developments had taken place, severely impacting the United States and its allies. A buddy of mine, who was scheduled to come home on the next transport ship was instead reassigned to Korea and I never heard from him again. I remained in California for about a month or so

PART 1: MEMOIRS

before transferring to *Lowry Air Force Base* in Denver, Colorado, to attend the *U.S. Air Force Supply School*. After graduating as a Supply Technician, I was assigned to the *Mt. Clemens Air Force Base,* just outside of Detroit, in Mt. Clemens, Michigan. I remained there for several months, working as a Corporal in base supply before being flown to Newfoundland, Canada, where I remained for about a year.

This was the beginning of the *Cold War* between the United States and its allies versus the Soviet Union and its allies. Both were fighting to win the territories of the newly developed nations of South America, Europe, Africa and Asia. After leaving Newfoundland, I was assigned to *Westover Air Force Base* in Chicopee, Massachusetts. I was given the option of re-enlisting or being discharged, in lieu of the additional year President Truman had tacked on to my original three-year enlistment. I chose the latter, which proved to work in my favor. Particularly, in light of a recent bill approved by Congress offering former Korean War veterans, the government educational assistance they needed to attend college.

PART 1: MEMOIRS

Ed and La Verne Meet

I was a 23-year-old struggling college student when I first met La Verne Rucks. Although I was an air force veteran, I was still relatively inexperienced in the area of romance. I had never really had a serious relationship before, particularly one that could lead to marriage. But when I met La Verne everything was different. As I have stated on many occasions to my children, I met their mother through the matchmaking efforts of Mrs. Urquhart—one of many customers I met while serving as a temporary mail carrier for the *McKeesport Post Office* in Pennsylvania.

Mrs. Urquhart was the mother of three daughters. One of her daughters was the same age as me, one was slightly younger, and one was slightly older. Although Mrs. Urquhart made numerous attempts at trying to match me with one of her daughters, it never worked. None of this appeared to phase Mrs. Urquhart, who seemed determined as ever to find me, as she called it, "A nice young girl who could be suitably paired with a nice boy like me."

One hot Summer day as I dropped off Mrs. Urquhart's mail, and sat briefly to enjoy a fresh glass of lemonade, she asked if I knew anyone in Liberty Borough. Liberty Borough was a residential area on the outskirts of

PART 1: MEMOIRS

McKeesport. I told her that I did not and she proceeded to describe La Verne in great detail.

According to my personal matchmaker, Mrs. Urquhart, La Verne was a very attractive, very religious girl who formerly attended Howard University in Washington, D.C. She was forced to interrupt her studies after hearing the news of her mother's sudden and unexpected passing. Apparently, La Verne had stayed behind to help her father who was in failing health himself and had yet to return to college.

Her description of La Verne sounded like someone I wanted to meet but, not wanting to appear desperate, I purposely did not take any immediate actions to inquire further. Mrs. Urquhart was not deterred by my apparent nonchalant attitude and became all the more persistent. One day, as I was dropping off her mail she appeared noticeably excited.

"La Verne is directing a play at her church," she said.

Providing me with La Verne's rehearsal times and schedule, she added that I might be able to catch one of the rehearsals after I finished my postal shift. I was hopeful that Mrs. Urquhart might have told La Verne about me as well. But when I finally broached the subject with La Verne, after

PART 1: MEMOIRS

we had gotten to know each other better, she always denied that Mrs. Urquhart had ever mentioned me to her.

The following week, I decided to end my shift early, so I could attend one of La Verne's practice sessions. I freshened up a bit and then walked to the church, arriving slightly after rehearsal had started. Sitting several rows in back of the practice area, I noticed a group of teenagers and pre-teens towards the center front of the church, practicing their lines. Off to the side stood this beautiful young woman instructing on what to do and how to do it. I was immediately awe struck by her physical beauty and the level of grace evident in the way she presented herself.

I had hoped that she would notice me, but she showed no signs of even turning in my direction. I felt a little throat clearing was in order to garner her attention and guess what? It worked! La Verne turned around and stared at me with a facial expression that begged to know who I was and why I was there.

"We are practicing for a play," she said.

"Are there any parts still available," I asked, "I might be interested in participating."

La Verne parried back with a comment on what I might want to do to participate. I advised her that I could read well, offering to do a reading for her. She seemed

PART 1: MEMOIRS

somewhat dubious about it but told me that I could be in the play; and to come back for the next practice, ready and prepared to do the reading I had proposed. I left the practice that day with my mind reflecting over several possible readings. For some odd reason, I locked in on the reading of, "How do I love thee." During the next practice session, I performed my reading. After the program, La Verne told me that the reading was not very good, most likely because I had not attended enough rehearsals.

Finally, the day had come for the performance of the play and my less than stellar performance. By this time, I was really interested in getting to know La Verne better. On the evening of the play, several of La Verne's friends—Dorothy White and Dorothy's father who was a Baptist minister—were in attendance. After the play, we engaged in bit of chit-chat. Rev. White's church was in the nearby community of Duquesne, Pennsylvania. He and Dorothy decided to offer La Verne a ride home. Noticing that I was hanging around the car, Rev. White asked:

"Young man, can I drop you off some place?"

In my mind, I wanted to say, "Yes, I want to go with you to La Verne's house!"

Instead, I gave him the address where I was staying. He dropped me off but I managed to get La Verne's

PART 1: MEMOIRS

telephone number before exiting the car. I did not hesitate to call her the next day and the next few days after that. She never turned down any of my calls but she put me off on agreeing to a date. She insisted on me first meeting her father. Her excuse for the delay was that the two of them were busy painting the house. I later learned, of course, that La Verne (who was not skilled in the slightest when it came to painting) was the one doing most of the painting.

My persistence finally paid off and I was invited to come to her house, meet her dad and have dinner with the two of them. It was the beginning of a loving and enduring relationship that would last nearly 60 years. It encompassed the birth of five children over a 10-year period; including moves from McKeesport to our first apartment in Pittsburgh, Pennsylvania, to Washington, D.C., Kensington, Maryland, Vestal, New York, Rockville, Maryland, Brookfield, Connecticut, Lawrenceville, New Jersey and finally to New Haven, Connecticut.

Together, these moves incorporate the span of my professional career. First, as a Radio News Reporter and Sports Announcer for the Pittsburgh radio station *WILY*. Secondly, as an Advertising Solicitor and Copy Writer for the *Pittsburgh Courier*. Thirdly, as a writer and reporter for the *U.S. Information Agency* in Washington, D.C. And

PART 1: MEMOIRS

finally, as a writer and Communications Manager for the *IBM* facilities in Maryland, New York, New Jersey and Connecticut.

La Verne was a consummate homemaker. She was always quick to make each house a home, getting rid of travel boxes and crates in record time. Our friends always marveled at how quickly all of our houses were easily transformed into a welcoming home.

PART 1: MEMOIRS

Proposal and Marriage

La Verne was employed at the *Irene Kaufman Center* in Pittsburgh when we first met. The center (which was only a couple of miles from my student base at Duquesne University), served as a recreational, cultural and social services outlet for at risk youths in the Hill Section of Pittsburgh. On occasion, I would drop by the center after my classes to spend time with La Verne until her shift ended. Afterwards, we would take the street car home to McKeesport—which was nearly a half-hour ride long—sharing our favorite candy (Chuckles) as we laughed and talked along the way. Sometimes La Verne would take the city bus in McKeesport, traveling alone to her home in Liberty Borough. At other times, I would take the city bus with her, walking back to my lodging.

It quickly became apparent to me that I had feelings for La Verne, feelings that were unlike anything I had ever felt before. She was physically attractive, very bright and had a great sense of humor; or at least I thought so since she laughed at all of my jokes. Without being consciously aware of what was going on, I found myself falling in love. As our relationship continued I found myself spending more time with La Verne, to the point of seeing her several times a

PART 1: MEMOIRS

week. Sometimes she would set aside a sandwich or hold a bit of leftovers for me from dinner. At other times, she did not bother to do anything, lest I take her and her kindness for granted.

On the occasions when we sat around watching television, we would send her cousin Mike out for some ice cream to avoid his prying eyes. If any money was left over from my GI check, after paying my tuition, I would take La Verne out for dinner. If we really wanted to splurge, we would venture up to the Point—the place where the Allegheny and Monongahela rivers met to form the Ohio River—where a new restaurant had been built as part of the City of Pittsburgh's redevelopment plan. Most of the time, La Verne and I were the only couple of color among the diners. None of this bothered us because we only had eyes for each other.

About six months or so into our relationship, I proposed to La Verne and she burst out in laughter because she knew I did not have enough money saved up to marry anyone, let alone her. In the subsequent weeks to follow, we had more in-depth conversations about a future life together, sharing information about our respective family histories and composition. I wrote to my mother, who was still living in West Virginia at that time, and told her I had found the

PART 1: MEMOIRS

girl I wanted to marry. Finally, on a beautiful moonlit night, in the Spring of 1954 and in the front yard of her home, La Verne agreed to become my wife. She asked me to talk to her dad to gain his approval. Without hesitation, I did this in rapid order. With Mr. Rucks' blessings, we immediately began planning our wedding. I eventually saved up enough money to purchase an engagement ring for La Verne, which I placed on her finger at one of our increasingly rare dinners.

I was working, at the time, in the *Pittsburgh Post Office* as a night shift mail clerk and sorter. La Verne and I agreed, since I was notoriously bad at saving money, that I would give her any money left over after I paid my basic living expenses. She, in turn, would deposit the money in a joint savings account for the two of us. We set the date of our wedding for the last day of December 1954, the same date that her best friend, Tookie, had gotten married several years prior.

In retrospect, this had to have been a very stressful time for La Verne. She was holding down a full-time job, helping take care of her dad, and planning a wedding with little help from anyone but her good friend, Gladdie, the wife of a local Baptist minister in town. Considerably older than La Verne, Gladdie looked at her as the younger sister or daughter she never had.

PART 1: MEMOIRS

Time seemed to move at warp speed and before I knew it, December was upon us and seemingly everything was moving at a hectic pace. The two of us had blood tests done. When the results came back, La Verne discovered that her blood had a Rh-negative factor. Initially, she was disturbed by the finding but the doctor assured us that it was nothing to be alarmed about as far as health and child bearing was concerned. Especially since I was Rh-positive with 'O' type blood.

We planned to hold our wedding at the local AME Zion church, where La Verne was a member. We thought we had her pastor's agreement in allowing Gladdie's husband (Rev. Harold Hayes) to be the officiating minister during our betrothal. But approximately two weeks prior to the wedding, her pastor (Rev. McClendon) threw a monkey wrench into our plans. He informed La Verne that he should rightfully be the officiate of our marriage and that Rev. Hayes could perform the marital vows. La Verne was highly upset over this last-minute change but we had no alternative than to accept it.

December 31, 1954—the day of our wedding—had finally come. La Verne's family was represented by her dad (who gave her away) and her cousin, Mike Turner. My side of the family was represented by my dad, his new wife,

PART 1: MEMOIRS

Minnie, along with several of my Pittsburgh cousins. My mother and siblings were unable to attend. My best man was Charles Russell (no relation), who was also a Duquesne student. La Verne's matron of honor was Regene Carmack of Cleveland, Ohio—someone she had grown extremely close to during their college days at Howard University.

We got through the "two-pastor" wedding ceremony and reception in the basement of the church without a glitch. Before leaving for our honeymoon at the Hilton Hotel at the Pittsburgh Airport, we accepted an invitation from our long-time friend, Rev. White, to attend Watch Night Service at his church in Duquesne, Pennsylvania.

We could not afford to take a flight anywhere, so we spent our honeymoon at the Greater Pittsburgh Airport Hotel; occasionally watching the flights take off and land from our hotel window and dreaming of all the flights we might one day take ourselves. Things get a little murky in my mind as to the chain of events that occurred after the watch night services. I seem to recall the entire wedding party joining us at the hotel, having some refreshments at the hotel bar and them eventually bidding us adieu, as La Verne and I checked into our hotel room for the weekend.

After our honeymoon, La Verne and I established temporary residence at the Rucks' home. Blinky, a fellow

PART 1: MEMOIRS

student from Duquesne University and a member of my wedding party was holding a few of my possessions in his car. Somehow, the picture folios of my family and years of military service were lost and never found. This was deeply disturbing to me because it meant that the limited photographlic record I had of my family and military life, was now gone forever. Notwithstanding this major disappointment, La Verne and I happily began our married life in the home she shared with her dad and cousin, Michael Turner, at 1031 Glenn Avenue in the Liberty Borough of McKeesport, Pennsylvania.

By the time we were married I was entering the second semester of my junior year at Duquesne University. I was hired as a Custodian and Night Watchman by one of the local department stores in McKeesport. La Verne continued her work at the Irene Kaufman Center. We both worked on our marriage but getting to know each other intimately was not so easy. Although I respected Mr. Rucks greatly, I was not comfortable living in his house. I vowed that as soon as I graduated from college and found another job that La Verne and I would find our own place. La Verne was deeply concerned about her dad's health but was not resistant to leaving since her cousin Mike was there to look

PART 1: MEMOIRS

out for him. At best, we probably would not leave for at least another year.

Sometime during the month of March 1955, La Verne informed me that she was pregnant. We were both excited and nervous about being parents to our first child. I still had a year of college to get through and our financial resources were less than ample. But the overwhelming emotion was one of happiness. After all, we were going to be first-time parents! We found a doctor that La Verne thought was wonderful, and her pregnancy proceeded without much difficulty or complaint. I, on the other hand, experienced sensations of morning sickness several times a week while riding the streetcar in route to school.

Our first child, Faith Cecelia, was born November 1, 1955 at McKeesport Hospital and I was a nervous wreck. A couple of weeks prior to Faith's arrival, I was seated next to someone who knew La Verne. While riding the streetcar to Pittsburgh, she rattled on and on about first-time pregnancies and how her sister had to be rushed to the hospital when her water broke because the baby was coming so fast. Water breaking? That was a totally foreign concept to me. So foreign, in fact, that I had to look it up.

Several days after the conversation, as I was preparing to leave for school when La Verne told me that she

PART 1: MEMOIRS

thought the baby was ready to come out. Not thinking anything of it, I naturally did not take her seriously. I knew that I had a short day at school that day and was fairly confident I would be home early enough before anything happened. Prior to me leaving, La Verne called her friend Gladdie. Gladdie, in turn, asked to speak with me, advising me to stay home on that day and I did.

Sometime during the day, La Verne's water broke and that got me super excited. I called a cab and worried that the baby's arrival was imminent. When the cab finally arrived, it seemed to take forever driving that short distance to the hospital. In those days, ether as the preferred drug that was administered to women giving birth. When the nurses finally informed me that I was the father of a new healthy baby girl, I could not wait to go in to see my wife. But somehow it seemed that every time La Verne opened her mouth to communicate, ether fumes would come spilling out leaving my head spinning and my stomach feeling woozy. Each time, I would have to leave the room to try and collect myself.

All was well with mother and daughter or, so we were told. But we were less than enthusiastic about the quality of services we received. La Verne required some minor stitching and the nursing support assigned to care for

PART 1: MEMOIRS

her was, in our opinion, not up to par. We took Faith to the pediatrician frequently during the early stages of her development but was never informed of any physiological problems she might be experiencing. We found that out sometime later after taking Faith to another doctor when she was in her pre-teens. The new doctor informed us that Faith had some amount of deformity with one of her legs but offered no satisfactory solution to correct it.

Everyone felt that Faith was a carbon copy of me. She had a full head of jet black hair with a small bald spot in the back of her head, which we concluded was due to how she slept in her crib. Whenever we took Faith to the doctor's office, I would sit her up on my lap in a way that would cover up the bald spot.

Faith was seven months old when I graduated in May 1956 from Duquesne University with a degree in Journalism. Unlike our wedding, my mother was able to attend the graduation. She and her new husband, Maceo, along with Webster Barnes (father-in-law of my sister Odessia) drove up from West Virginia. La Verne had them over for breakfast before they drove to Pittsburgh for the graduation ceremonies. La Verne laid out a nice spread, including assorted Danish. In return for all her efforts, the following comment was made: *"We don't eat sweet bread in the*

PART 1: MEMOIRS

morning." We did not have any biscuits or corn bread to offer them, so assorted Danish it was.

I left early on the day of graduation, taking the streetcar into Duquesne University, to take care of some last-minute matters. La Verne, Faith and Mr. Rucks had planned to ride with my friend, Charles, to the graduation; followed by mom and Maceo riding in Mr. Barnes car. Things got pretty dicey prior to the graduation. My mother had a big tear in her stockings and Charles volunteered to take her into town to get another pair. It had been raining that day and the section of Glenn Road where Mr. Rucks lived was unpaved. On the way back, Charles' car got stuck in a ditch with my mother inside his car. It took some effort on his part but he was finally able to free the car and get back to the house.

Meanwhile, La Verne was growing anxious and concerned they all would be late for my graduation. Good news is, everyone made it there safe and in time to see me graduate. It was the first time my mother and La Verne had met, so I was pleased that everything went reasonably well. But I was also relieved when the three of them finally left to go back home, that is, after stuffing themselves on some more of La Verne's good cooking.

To my dismay, there was more calamity to come. Shortly after mom, Maceo and Mr. Barnes had left, we

PART 1: MEMOIRS

received a call from them informing us that their car had broken down in Connellsville, Pennsylvania near the West Virginia line. I did not have a car or AAA membership, so there was little I could do to help them. Somehow, they found a way to resolve their issues and make their way back home.

After I graduated, I was able to find employment right away as a News and Sports Announcer with Radio Station WILY in Pittsburgh. Their programming focused primarily on the city's African American community. Although my journalism degree concentrated on print reporting, advertising and public relations, I was happy to take on the job of a radio news announcer. Based on the feedback received from the station's listening audience, they were equally pleased to have me serving in this capacity.

It was the practice of the Station Manager to use some of the Staff Disc Jockeys to report the news throughout the day. Sorely lacking any real journalism skills, the jockeys frequently butchered pronunciations and generally made a mockery of any news reporting. Many in the African American community, including the Pittsburgh branch of the NAACP protested to station management that these news broadcasts were offensive and insulting. The Station Manager had been under pressure to find someone trained in

PART 1: MEMOIRS

news reporting and I happened to be the only black journalism graduate in Pittsburgh at that time.

So, when the Station Manager called the Journalism Department at Duquesne University, it resulted in three happy people—me, my journalism coordinator (who prided himself on successfully placing graduates in jobs) and the Station Manager from WILY in Pittsburgh, who was in desperate need. After a week at the radio station, I became known as Russ Russell, WILY News and Sports Announcer; and La Verne and I began discussing the move from her dad's house in McKeesport to an apartment in Pittsburgh.

PART 1: MEMOIRS

La Verne and Mom

La Verne and mom were raised under similar circumstances in their early youth. As La Verne began to slowly reveal more of her family background to me, the similarities between the two only served to strengthen her appeal. Growing up in New Kensington and McKeesport Pennsylvania, La Verne was under the impression that her grandparents (Cecelia and John Rucks) were actually her mother and father. There were two older daughters in the family, Irma and Thelma. La Verne had always imagined that she was their youngest daughter. However, at the age of 12 or 13, La Verne was told by her two older sisters they were actually her mother and aunt.

According to La Verne, she was not entirely shocked by this revelation. She made a point of explaining to everyone that she would continue to regard her grandparents as her true parents because they had taken the initiative to raise her. Thelma, La Verne's birth mother, was married to a young dentist named Russell Lewis when La Verne was born. Shortly after La Verne's birth, the couple broke up, with Russell fading from the scene, never to be heard from again. Somehow, the decision was made that Mr. And Mrs. Rucks would raise La Verne as their own daughter. Thelma

PART 1: MEMOIRS

eventually left home and moved to New York, where she worked in the field of social services for the remainder of her life. Irma also left home and made New York her home after getting married, having a son and settling down in a suburban community called Crestwood.

La Verne never had the pleasure of meeting her birth father in real life. As I recall, she made several attempts to reach out to him after the two of us got married and had settled in Maryland to raise our family. However, I also recall La Verne telling me that on the one occasion the two of them spoke by phone, he sounded extremely nervous after she had identified herself. The conversation was rather awkward and ended with him making a false promise to get back in touch with her at some later date. Of course, that phone call never took place and La Verne never tried to reach out to him again. She did, however, remain in touch with her birth mother, Thelma, until her death. After La Verne and I got married, the family lost contact with Irma. But her son, Michael, eventually moved to McKeesport to live with his grandparents, Mr. And Mrs. Rucks.

My mother, like La Verne, was not raised by her birth mother or father but instead was brought up by foster parents. Neither of them knew their birth father and, in my mother's case, she never knew her mother either. Although

PART 1: MEMOIRS

my mother never admitted it, I personally believe, the lack of knowledge of her personal history created a void in her heart that she never got over. It was fairly obvious to me that it bothered her all throughout her life.

La Verne seemed to have a very warm spot in her heart for my mother. Mostly, I think, because she understood and empathized with the life she was forced to live as an orphan. As such, La Verne was instrumental in helping me to get through some of the rough patches in my relationship with my mother.

PART 1: MEMOIRS

Fatherhood

Of all the gifts La Verne gave me during our life together, the most precious was the gift of fatherhood. When I first fell in love with La Verne, I envisioned the day when we would eventually become parents. I am the first to admit that I did not think we would reach the number five but with the birth of the twins, we leapfrogged from three children to five. As the old saying goes, "the pencil broke and that's all she wrote."

You can draw your own conclusions but I think it is safe to say that after having five children in ten years, La Verne and I learned more about family planning and practicing what you plan. The two of us felt that each of our children, planned or not, was a true blessing. Since neither of us were raised in traditional households with a mother and father, so our parenting skills developed on a day-to-day basis. We also learned a great deal about child rearing from our family bible, authored by the famed Dr. Benjamin Spock.

Unlike other married couples, we did not look to the bible to choose our children's names. *Faith Cecelia* is the given name of our first daughter. She was named *Faith* because it seemed appropriate to our finances at the time.

PART 1: MEMOIRS

Our finances were meager back then but we believed by "faith" that He would bring us through it all and He did. Faith's middle name, *Cecelia*, was derived from La Verne's grandmother.

Bridgette Patrice, our second daughter, came along at a time when Africans were shedding their colonial rule in lieu of becoming independent nations. The French actress, Brigitte Bardot, was the reigning star in film and television. So, we chose the name *Bridgette* as our daughter's first name, with a slightly different spelling from the famed actress. Bridgette's second name was derived from African revolutionary, Patrice Lumumba, who was killed in the struggle, while trying to form a majority rule government in what is now called Zaire.

Lisa Millicent was the name chosen for our third daughter. La Verne and I both readily agreed on our daughter's middle name being *Millicent* as it was also La Verne's middle name. But we had considerable discussion on her first name before finally settling on *Lisa*. La Verne's original choice was Belinda but her cousin, Anna, sided in favor of the name Lisa. Plus, we both liked the idea of La Verne and Lisa sharing the same initials (LMR).

La Verne took the lead in naming our twin sons. The first to be born would be named *Edgar III*, after me and my

PART 1: MEMOIRS

father. The second to be born would be named *John*, after both of our grandfathers. We later added the middle name of *Rucks* to John's name, in honor of La Verne's maiden name.

La Verne worked very hard on nurturing the love of family. We recognized the individuality of each of our children with their distinct personalities. And we wanted each of them to develop to his and her potential while also being quick and proud to support the achievements of their siblings. That, to us, is what family is all about and we were pleased and blessed to see this concept take hold with our children and our grandchildren. It's an integral part of our legacy.

PART 1: MEMOIRS

Thoughts on La Verne

During a luncheon meeting with Rev. Robinson (who at the time was the Pastor of First Baptist Church), I mentioned the idea of me writing a memoir of my life. He suggested that I might want to write about my feelings and thoughts after La Verne died. He was of the opinion that it might be useful as a matter of recollection for our children. Not wanting to rob my children and others of their own personal feelings about La Verne—a beloved wife, mother and friend—this is my attempt to capture my feelings and thoughts about her during the last weeks and months of her life.

From the moment she was hospitalized, following her fall in our Spring Meadows apartment, until the first few weeks of her stay at Cambridge Health and Rehabilitation Center, I wavered between hopeful optimism and dreadful doubt that La Verne might or might not recover. I consider myself blessed to have had a very resilient family, who seemed determined in their fight to do everything possible to restore La Verne's health. It helped to strengthen me in fighting off the occasional demons of doubt that periodically dominated my thoughts.

PART 1: MEMOIRS

The first couple of weeks during La Verne's stay at Cambridge, the staff doctor and I played phone tag. When we finally did connect, I was totally unprepared to digest what he was about to tell me. Everyone in the family was prayerfully and confidently optimistic about her eventual recovery. Listening to his rather abrupt matter-of-fact tone of voice, which insisted she only had about six months to live, was a real shocker. I was rendered nearly speechless and quite honestly did not know how to react. I managed to utter a few innocuous verbal responses to his suggestion that we consider putting La Verne in hospice care.

When I later proposed the idea to our children (leaving out some of the more important details), they all seemed quite adamant that they were not buying into the finality of her situation. I discovered somewhat later that the doctor had had a similar conversation with one of our daughters, hoping to defuse any non-acceptance of his premise that there was little chance that La Verne could or would eventually get better. Although there are always differences of opinion among family members in cases like these, I thought it important that we stick together as a family in having one voice.

Despite the few good and responsive days that La Verne experienced, she became increasingly incapable of following her prescribed rehabilitation over the ensuing weeks. Neither did she accept, in any significant amounts, the nourishment needed to sustain her efforts. As the demons of doubt slowly crept back into my mind, I found myself praying more often and frequently, as did every other member of our family. The biggest blow for me was when La Verne became verbally non-responsive. The moment this happened, I had basically one resolve: I did not want the end of life to come with her hooked up to all kinds of machines. If her death was destined to be, then I wanted it to be as natural and humane as possible.

Shortly after one of my latter visits to the *Cambridge Rehabilitation Center and Nursing Home*, La Verne suffered a relapse. The nursing staff at Cambridge contacted the nearest hospital, dispatching La Verne by ambulance while calling me. The day prior to her relapse had been one of her most peaceful days yet. She seemed at ease and was breathing well. I remember leaving the hospital that evening feeling a sense of ease and positive thoughts. However, when I got to the hospital and saw La Verne hooked up to a respirator, with the nurses and doctors scurrying in and out of her room, I was disheartened again. I knew within my heart that this was not how she would have wanted her end-of-life experience to be.

PART 1: MEMOIRS

One of the staff doctors at the hospital strengthened my resolve by sharing some of the steps he went through when his father was diagnosed with a similar condition as La Verne. I was informed that La Verne was in the end stages of dementia. With that diagnosis in mind, my next step was to rid La Verne of all the devices attached to her, allow her to breathe on her own, sign her into hospice care and return her back to Cambridge. I thanked God that the family was unanimously on board with the decision.

Prior to La Verne's admission into hospice care and before my last visit to the hospital, I had established a daily routine of pushing La Verne in her wheelchair through the rehab facility corridors and around the outside perimeter of the facility. During the early to mid-stages of these daily rendezvous, the attendants would have La Verne up and ready to go at the agreed time. She would often be sitting in the chair waiting for me and would greet me with that lovely smile when she heard my voice.

During our early daily wheelchair rides I talked endlessly and La Verne listened—a dramatic change from the times when she was the talker and I was more of a listener. Over the last few weeks of our time together, I noticed a sharp decline in her mental sharpness and receptiveness to things. She became increasingly lethargic and yet I could tell she was fighting hard to remain as responsive as she could until the end.

While under hospice care, she was no longer connected to any machines. Instead, she was connected to the tender loving care of nurses, who were spiritually motivated, compassionate, sensitive, prayerful and kind. This renewed my faith and belief that we made the right decision in bringing Hospice into the picture. Now, I was dealing with a new reality: I could no longer wheel La Verne around in her wheelchair, which meant that she and I would no longer have any future wheelchair dates.

I knew that living out one's days in a hospice would have an end time. But when that day actually came, no one (least of all me) was prepared to accept my wife's death. Honestly, is anyone ever really prepared for the end? My mind understood the reality of the situation, but my heart did not. As a Christian, I believe there is life after the death of our physical bodies and possible reunification in a spiritual realm. But I could not help but grieve over the loss of my life companion.

She was 10 years old when she dedicated her life to Christ. Her faith was as solid as the hardest rock. She was the kind of woman who not only talked the life but walked in the fullness of that life. She was the mother of my

PART 1: MEMOIRS

children, someone who truly believed our marriage was a sacred covenant between us and God. She knew me better than I even knew myself. At this very moment, I want to be selfish. I do not want to see her go or let her go. I know that life and death go hand-in-hand. And yes, I have lost other people—my mother, father, two sisters, a brother and grandparents too. But nothing compares to the pain of me losing La Verne. It is the deepest most sorrowful pain I have ever felt in my entire life.

In subsequent days and weeks following La Verne's interment, I felt (still feel) as if a critical part of me is missing. When I am in bed, I can still feel her lying next to me. When I wake up, I can still hear her breathing and softly calling my name. There are times when I wonder why God did not choose to take me at the same time. I knew it is a selfish thought but it would have been nice if we could have entered into eternity together. During those moments of human frailty, I can also hear the voice of Truth speaking as He reminds me: *"Edgar, think about your children, grandchildren and great grandchildren. How would they feel if they were to endure the loss of both of you at the very same time?"*

God has chosen to keep me here for a reason. I am learning to be grateful for all the times La Verne and I shared

PART 1: MEMOIRS

on this earthly plain. Most of all, I am thankful and grateful to God for all the blessings bestowed upon our family. I will continue to pray that, when my journey here is over, La Verne and I will find ourselves in each other's arms, rekindling all the memories and love that has stood the test of time.

PART 1: MEMOIRS

Mom as a Mother

My mom was great when it came to her being my mom. But she was not so great when it came to her being a mother. She never shied from the fact that she was our birth mother but when it came to her skills in nurturing, guiding and providing unconditional love to each of her children without deference, she often fell short of our expectations. I confess that I had a very troubled relationship with my mother, starting in my late teens into my early young adult life. I have to give credit to my wife, La Verne, for helping me to understand and make certain allowances for what I regarded as my mother's shortcomings.

As I matured into my role as a father, I began to see my mother in a less judgmental way, which led to significant improvements in our relationship. As a child, I felt she frequently showed favoritism among her children. More often than not, Ida and I (her two oldest children) got the short end of the stick. We were often blamed for things when things went wrong and received little to no credit when things went right.

Mom also had a color problem—a secret prejudice that she kept well-hidden even though it showed itself from time to time. In her mind, the closer you were in skin color

PART 1: MEMOIRS

to her light brown skin tone, the better. Ida was too fair and I was too dark. Altogether, we were a very competitive family. Mom liked to play us off one another, trying to keep us at odds with one another. Roland and I became her prime victims. Regardless of whether the two of us were singing, dancing, drawing or simply telling jokes, she would inevitably dub Roland as the winner. We both knew that there were times when Roland was the actual winner. However, there were also far too many times when he was not. The intentional rivalry imposed upon us embittered me greatly and I ultimately became a sore loser.

As an adult and parent, I came to a place where I learned to appreciate my mom for what she was—a single mother of five who never abandoned us. Keeping things in perspective as a child was extremely difficult because my mother often made us feel responsible for the hardships she had to bear. She had a split personality in that some days, she would be perfectly loving, engaging, humorous and full of the joy of life. Not long afterwards, she would spiral out of control into the depths of deep depression. (Had La Verne been exposed to any of this, she would have definitely recommended that my mother seek counseling).

Occasionally, a bottle of whiskey would calm her down, creating a false sense of happiness and joy. But this

PART 1: MEMOIRS

was generally followed by a period of deep despair prior to her falling asleep, as her children stood by anxiously waiting for the event to occur. In between my mother's separation from my dad, and prior to her marrying Maceo, there were many men in my mother's life. We routinely hated them all, except for one guy who we all liked and expressed our admiration for to mom. We never saw him again.

None of us understood our mother's choices for male companionship. And frankly, I am convinced she did not either. In retrospect, mom probably would have fared better if she had stayed in school instead of choosing to get married and starting a family before she was ready to become a mother. Then again, when all is said and done, everything falls within God's timing and plan. I pray that her soul is resting in peace.

PART 1: MEMOIRS

Dad as a Father

The kindest thing I can say about my dad in relation to him being a father, provider and proven example of family life and interaction is that he was "missing in action" most of the time. Once he and mom separated, he did not bother to keep in touch with any of his children. Outside of the few months my dad lived with his father before moving to Pittsburgh, Roland and I did not have much contact with him either. As all of my siblings and I grew into our teens, we only saw him on rare and fleeting occasions over the course of the next eight years. Our only consistent contact with him was through an occasional letter. But when it came to him being physically present in the flesh, he was more of a stranger to us than a father.

Ironically, I never thought of him as a bad person. Instead, I was somewhat sympathetic towards him when it came to his failings. I simply understood the dynamics of our relationship in that biologically he was my dad but realistically he never performed much like a father. Years after I graduated from high school, I went to live with dad in Pittsburgh, Pennsylvania, while I worked and saved up money for college. Dad and I did a lot of talking back then, which allowed me to get to know him better.

PART 1: MEMOIRS

Like me, my older sister, Ida, got to know dad later in life after she had married. He visited her in Brooklyn, New York to meet her daughter and his granddaughter, Debby. He also visited me several times to meet our children when we lived in Maryland. He hit it off with my wife and told me more than once that I was not the only Edgar to love La Verne.

Ida, it seemed, had it her mind to reunite mom and dad as a couple. She spent a lot of time plotting to try and get them back together again. I did not share her enthusiasm in this regard because both of my parents had already established new families for themselves. The irony of it all is dad would frequently proclaim that mom was the only woman he ever loved, although I personally never saw any evidence of it.

During the two summers I spent with him (1947-1948), I discovered that my dad was basically a quiet even-tempered type of man, who read a lot and enjoyed keeping up with world events. He did not smoke but had a fondness for chewing tobacco. He was not much of a drinker but frequented places that served alcoholic beverages, where he could hook up with some unattached female.

I remember telling him once, "Dad, you're looking for love in all the wrong places." Afterwards, I would tell

PART 1: MEMOIRS

him about the lady I met at Bethlehem Baptist Church who always asked about him; but dad was never interested in any "church lady," as he called it. He was extremely proud (at the age of 50) that he had finally secured the type of employment that provided health coverage and a pension. He was as a Custodian for the McKeesport office of the Pennsylvania Department of Social Services. When I moved to Pennsylvania to attend college, after leaving the military, he insisted on introducing me to his supervisor. I recall the supervisor telling me how grateful they all were for dad's dedicated service, observing *"Never has this facility been kept so clean."* I remember looking down at the sparkling floors and feeling warmth toward my dad in that moment.

PART 1: MEMOIRS

Family Tree of Siblings

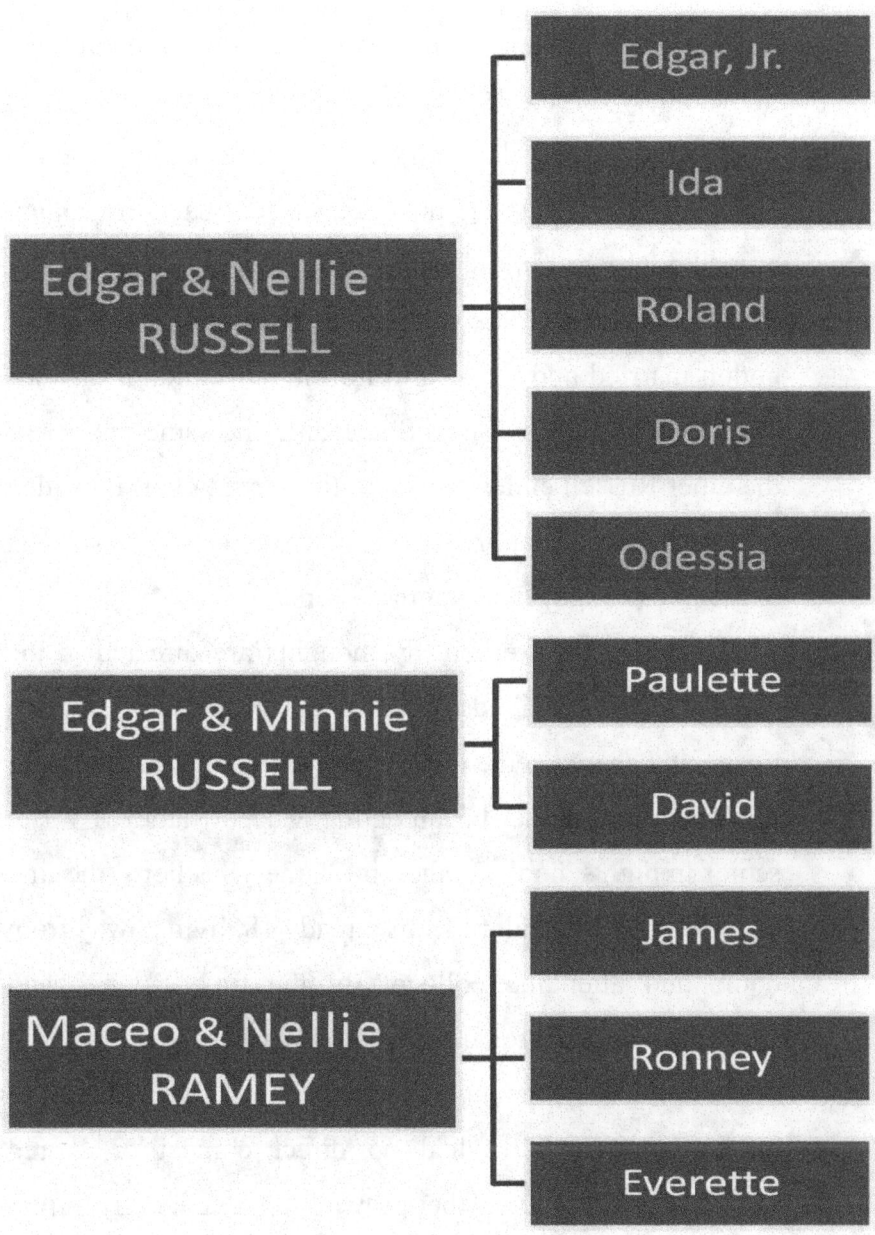

PART 1: MEMOIRS

Siblings

When I think about my siblings, my thoughts are immediately directed to the first to come out of the union between mom and dad, which was me, Roland, Odessia, Doris and Ida. Dad was not Odessia's actual birth father, even though we always regarded her as one of the Russell kids. We became aware of this sometime after Odessia had gotten married and decided to inform her children that she was not a Russell by birth. She shared the same mother as the other Russell children but not the same father. I decided to share this information with my children myself as opposed to them learning it from another source.

I think the reason my thoughts are directed to the original five Russell kids first is because we were the closest in age and shared some of the same experiences in growing up. When my mother began dating Maceo Ramey, I was a senior in high school. By the time James was born (the first to come from this union) I was already 18, living away from home and attending college. By the time Ronney and Everette Ramey were born several years later, I was serving in the U.S. Air Force. Although I regard them all as my brothers, we actually had no direct contact or shared experience with one another growing up; due largely in part to the age difference between us, which inhibited the level of the closeness experienced between me and the other Russell children.

I also have another sister and brother (Paulette and David) from dad's union with a woman named Minnie, (I never knew her last name). The two of them coupled up after mom and dad separated. I can literally count on one hand the number of times I have seen Paulette or David. Their mother discouraged any contact between them and the original Russell children and she was extremely successful in her efforts. Since dad's death in 1977, I have had periodic thoughts of reestablishing contact with them, to the point of making a few unsuccessful efforts to contact Paulette by phone. Before the passing of my Aunt JoAnn, she informed me that dad's family in Pittsburg (his nieces and nephews) had not been in contact with Paulette or David and had no relationship with them. The last known residence for Paulette was somewhere in McKeesport, Pennsylvania; and David's whereabouts are yet to be determined although he is rumored to have been incarcerated at some point.

Even if I were to somehow manage to get in contact with the two of them, I am not certain what could be accomplished from it. Both would be somewhere in their late fifties to early sixties by now and beyond the fact that we

PART 1: MEMOIRS

share bloodlines, there really would be no point in us connecting given we have no common heritage. Plus, they might very well feel as though they were breaching their mother's trust if they were to actually have any contact with us. When I had thoughts of possibly reaching out to them to reconnect, La Verne would tell me, "Russ, better to let sleeping dogs sleep."

PART 1: MEMOIRS

La Verne's Poem

When I think of major losses during my life
My thoughts come quickly to the passing of my wife.

Our journey in this world is for a relatively short time
But I never thought her life would end before mine.

I miss her lovely smile and the special way
she looked at me
That without too much effort on her part
put me on a path to ecstasy.

I miss her empathy and genuine sympathy
for anyone in need.
Both were core parts of her creed.

To me she was a rare jewel
That must be treasured like a Spiritual renewal.

Her love and trust were given from the heart
As true at the end as it was from the start.

PART 1: MEMOIRS

Instinct

In his book, Instinct: The Power to Unleash Your Inborn Drive, famed Author, Pastor and Entrepreneur, Bishop T. D. Jakes speaks at length concerning the power to unleash human inner drive and instincts. He is quoted to have said, "Following your instincts will transform your workplace, liberate your career and enhance your relationships." Often times, this drive is held back by an opposing force called practicality. We want to do the safe thing and sure thing that protects us from failure. However, taking "risk-free" steps seldom get us to the same place where our unbridled instincts can. This leaves us yearning for more when we look at our life accomplishments: Have I exercised my talents fully? Have I derived from this vessel, all that it can offer? These are some of the unanswered questions that arise when practicality dominates our lives.

Inventors, explorers, innovators, scientist, artists and high achievers, in nearly every field of endeavor, have been known to constantly push the envelope against the status quo. They are the ones who are unafraid to ask why, why not and what if. Today, we have access to volumes of information on almost every subject. And yet, we allow empirical data to cloud our judgment and enslave us with a

PART 1: MEMOIRS

sense of practicality that muzzles our instincts and pursuits on new horizons.

Robert Kennedy once said, "Only those who dare to fail greatly can ever achieve greatly."[1] Bishop T. D. Jakes said, "All that matters in this brief vacation we take on earth is that we don't shrink into a corner and waste the days were given doing what we have to do rather than rising and taking on the challenge of becoming all that we were created to be."[2] A great example of someone who chose to liberate themselves from practicality and doing only what is expected of them is former POTUS, George H.W. Bush. In honor of his 90th birthday, this 41st President found the courage to parachute out of a plane. I do not mean to suggest that we should allow our instincts to drive us to engage in dangerous actions but I do firmly believe that for some it may be a source of relief and deviation from a "strait-jacketed" lifestyle to a liberating one that inspires a zest for life and exploration.

---

[1] Robert Kennedy Quotes. (n.d.). BrainyQuote.com. Retrieved from https://www.brainyquote.com/quotes/robert_kennedy_101795.

[2] Jakes, Bishop T.D. (2014). *Instinct: The Power to Unleash Your Inborn Drive.* TDJ Enterprises, LLP. FaithWords, a division of Hachette Book Group: New York.

PART 2:

MISCELLANEOUS RAMBLINGS

PART 3: REFLECTIONS

Mr. Miller: "A Child of Slavery and a Hero"

The year was 1863, one week after President Abraham Lincoln's signing of the Emancipation Proclamation, abolishing slavery. Newly freed Negroes on plantations from Virginia to Mississippi celebrated the good news. Among those celebrating was Jakub Miller, 17, and his new bride, Amantha, 16. Both were slaves on the southwestern Tennessee tobacco plantation owned by Robert G. Miller, the same slave owner that Jakub had derived his last name from.

The young couple had good reason for celebrating, not only because of their newly acquired freedom but also because of the promise from Mr. Miller that they could live on the land rent free as sharecroppers: *"Yawl got your freedom now and I don't own you anymore,"* their owner informed them shortly after the proclamation. *"I'm going to sell off most of the plantation but I plan to keep about a third of it as a source of steady income. I'm offering you to stay on the land rent free as sharecroppers. Yawl can keep a third of any profit made from our tobacco crop. I have no heirs, so when I die the land will be turned over to you."* The young couple looked at each with excitement before agreeing to accept his offer.

PART 3: REFLECTIONS

As former sharecroppers, Jakub and Amantha proved to be successful tobacco farmers. When Mr. Miller died in 1875, he left his remaining property to Jakub and Amantha as promised. Ten years later, at age of 26 and 27, the young couple found themselves owners of a 200-acre plot of land, which they continued to farm for the next 20 years. In 1895, an unexpected event occurred that shocked them both. Now in their late forties, Amantha was pregnant. On November 5, 1895, the first and only child, George Singapore Miller was born. Dark-skinned like his parents with sparkling brown eyes, young George showed early signs that he was gifted. He learned to walk before he was one year old. By the age of six, he had a fully functional vocabulary and was reading and writing at a sixth-grade level by the time he was seven.

Jakub and Amantha did everything they could, within the constraints of the segregated society, to keep young George intellectually stimulated and challenged. They were frequent visitors to the colored section of the local library, checking out literary classics and books on world history, science and geography. In 1911, at the age of 16, George graduated at the top of his class from a segregated high school for colored students. His parents used their considerable savings to send him to Lincoln University in

PART 3: REFLECTIONS

Philadelphia, Pennsylvania—one of the land grant colleges that were set up after the civil war to provide a post high school learning environment for former slaves and their descendants. In 1915, George Miller graduated from Lincoln University at the top of his class.

In those days, the opportunities for a college educated Black man in Tennessee were practically non-existent beyond that of manual labor. George quickly found himself searching for work in the booming coal mining territory of West Virginia, settling in Bramwell—home to a growing number of affluent coal mining operators and owners.

Coal was king in those days and there was high demand for workers to go down into the bowels of the earth to bring the "black gold" to the surface for processing. A segment of those answering this demand for minors included both Black migrants from the south and White immigrants from Europe. George became a part of a small group of vanguard Black professionals and merchants, who coalesced in and around Bramwell, to offer support services for the Black workers and their families who were mushrooming throughout the area.

At the age of 23, George became the only paid employee of the local Black Masonic Lodge. He also

PART 3: REFLECTIONS

intermittently served as the Justice of the Peace, performing marriages on behalf of the town's colored population. Attired in a stiff-necked, freshly starched white shirt and dark suit seven days a week, George stood out among both the Black and White town folks of Bramwell. Known for his precise diction and quick wit, he was different. He commanded respect and soon became the un-elected leader of the colored community and unofficial ambassador between the White and Black segments of the population.

Although he never enjoyed many of the constitutional rights afforded to his White counterparts, this son of slaves did his best (within the 65 years of his life) to live out the American dream. A staunch Baptist, George was quick to attribute his success to his Christian faith, Abraham Lincoln and the Republican party in general. By the time he was 28 years old, he had already built and occupied a pre-fabricated home with two bedrooms, a living room, dining room, kitchen and bathroom—a rare feat for men of his age and even more so for a Black man in his day.

A mere 5'5' in height, George stood much taller in the esteem of those who knew him. As one of the fortunate few who benefitted from his wisdom, during my years of growing up, he was an inspirational giant who inculcated in me the belief that are four pathways to success in life:

PART 3: REFLECTIONS

Keeping faith, studying hard, being disciplined, and maintaining a healthy dose of aspiration.

Despite the many accomplishments of great and notable African-Americans and their contributions in the arts, academics, religion, politics, world affairs and sports, when I think of who my greatest hero is, I always think of Mr. George Miller.

PART 3: REFLECTIONS

She Is With Me

A Love Poem

In the dawn of day
She rises with me.
As I go my way
She goes with me.

In the dark of night
When I lie in bed
She is with me.

As I rest my head
She is with me.
When I go to sleep
She is with me.

Dear to my heart
As she was from the start
She is with me.

Gone from here to eternity
I see.
But she is still with me.

PART 3: REFLECTIONS

A Memorable Drive

"Nothing like an open-air drive in the woods on a beautiful day. I'm so glad we bought the convertible," Jessica said, as she and Harry sped along a country road.

"Looks like some kind of road block up ahead" Harry responded.

No sooner than he had spoken the words, Harry heard several sirens coming behind them and immediately pulled over to the curb.

"I wonder what's going on?" Harry said.

Several emergency response vehicles, including a police car, ambulance and fire truck went speeding by.

"I hope it's not a bad accident," Jessica said.

"If it is then I'm afraid we're going to be stuck here for quite a while with the road being so narrow," Harry replied. "There's little room to move traffic around if the accident is really bad."

The cars ahead of them had come to a complete stop. Harry and Jessica were still too far off to see what the actual problem was. But it was a warm day and the once soothing breeze they had experienced while riding in the convertible was now still, stifling and becoming very uncomfortable.

PART 3: REFLECTIONS

"It's hot" Jessica lamented. "I hope we're not going to be here too long."

"Me too," Harry replied. "But we do have some cd's. I'll turn on the air conditioning for a while and we can relax while listening to some music."

Though a good idea, their listening was short-lived and quickly interrupted by the siren of an *Animal Rescue and Wildlife Services* vehicle that sped by.

"What in the heck is going on," Harry asked. "I've never seen this variety of emergency vehicles together all at the same time."

People in cars ahead of them had begun exiting their vehicles and walking towards the road block, ignoring the bull horn of pleas from emergency workers to stay in their cars until given the "all clear" signal. Curiosity eventually got the best of Jessica and Harry too and they quickly found themselves venturing out from their cars as well. There were at least a dozen cars in front of them.

As they inched their way closer to the cause of the road block, they were in for the surprise of their lives. A farmer had been leading a herd of cows into the meadow on the other side of the road when one very pregnant member of the herd was forced to succumb to the call of mother nature, giving birth right in the middle of the road.

PART 3: REFLECTIONS

Jessica and Harry arrived just in time to see the mother and her newborn calf arise from their labor and saunter off into the nearby meadow. City people, who had never witnessed an animal giving birth up close and personal, considered it one of the most memorable experiences of their lives, as did Jessica and Harry.

PART 3: REFLECTIONS

A Memorable Outing

"Don't go near the stream!" La Verne shouted.

"Neither of you know how to swim and I don't know how deep the water is," she said, as Edgar and John played on a nearby river bank.

Her six-year-old twin boys were racing along the river bank, excited over their first day at camp in the woods. It was a long-awaited dream that their dad had promised to them and they were determined to make the most of it. Their sisters, Lisa (9), Bridgette (12) and Faith (15), were less enthusiastic than their brothers but nevertheless welcomed the new adventure. The family had never camped out before. They eagerly joined their dad in selecting a campsite located a few yards from the river bank, blanketed on either side by a set of tall trees.

"We'll be able to get all the sun we want while at the same time providing a bit of shade," Ed thought to himself, as he unhitched the trailer and began to erect the pop-up tent in the clearing between the trees.

"Hey kids, come help me!" he called out.

Edgar considered the effort of putting up the tent a family project. He was already convinced that setting it up properly would take more time than the salesman had

PART 3: REFLECTIONS

previously eluded to. After a few trials and errors, the tent stood majestically before them awaiting their entrance. Setting up the cots was a much easier project, as they all imagined what it would be like to sleep among the trees, under the night stars, while listening to the tranquil sounds of the nearby river.

But first there was the little matter of preparing dinner. The kids gathered up some twigs and branches as kindling for the campfire. To this, Ed added some store bought wooden logs, creating the type of campfire that would eventually cook their baked beans, franks and burgers. If the campfire failed to work out as planned, then Ed was prepared to pull out the Japanese Hibachi cooking stove he had bought along for the trip. He could imagine the smell of the homemade pancakes La Verne would make, in her large mixing bowl, the following morning.

As it turned out, everything worked as planned. The food was great and had a special outdoor taste or, at least that is what everyone imagined and believed. Tidbits of burger were occasionally dropped into the birdcage for Agnes, their pet parrot, which their oldest daughter Brigette had insisted that they bring along. Of course, Agnes enhanced the family experience by chattering all throughout the family mealtime. The only thing that went awry was the discovery that they

PART 3: REFLECTIONS

had somehow forgotten to pack the can of tennis balls that was meant to benefit their daughters who were novice to the game.

"You can still use the camp tennis courts," La Verne said to her daughters, "You'll just have to rent balls from the attendants."

After a few campfire songs and some old, mostly unfunny jokes from Ed (who imagined himself to be a comedian), everyone except Faith entered the tent for the night. Faith, who wanted to experience the joys of sleeping in a sleeping bag on the ground outside, quickly realized that it was not all that it was cracked up to be. Just as the family settled down in their cots within the comforts of the tent, there was a frightening and somewhat panicky knock on the canvas door. It was Faith. She had heard an undecipherable noise outside and decided she would much rather sleep in the tent with the rest of the family.

Around 2:00 a.m., the family was awakened by several loud claps of thunder and streaks of lightning. Suddenly, the idea of sleeping among the trees did not sound like such a good idea. The rain came in torrents.

"Ed we're rather close to the creek and this rain could be a problem," La Verne suggested. "Maybe we ought to move out just to be on the safe side."

PART 3: REFLECTIONS

"Honey it just started raining. I'm sure it's going to stop soon," Ed said, in an assuring tone.

Fifteen minutes later, it was still raining and the sound of the creek was becoming louder as its waters became increasingly choppy.

"Ed, I think we should move to higher ground," La Verne shouted with a sense of urgency.

Before Ed could respond, the beam of a flashlight invaded their tent, competing with the periodic lightning flashes.

"This is an emergency!" a voice cried out in the darkness. "We are requesting that all campers move to the camp hall on the hill due to possible flash flooding! I repeat, this is an emergency! All campers move to the camp hall on the hill due to possible flash flooding."

La Verne quickly exchanged a glance at Ed, as if to say, "I told you so." Meanwhile, everyone quickly got up and started getting dressed in their rain gear. Now safely at the camp hall, they stared at the sights below as the once small stream became an angry growling body of water that was surging closer to the camping site they recently occupied. They would have a lot to talk about when they got home, for it had indeed been a memorable outing.

PART 3: REFLECTIONS

A Pistol Packing Christmas

I can recall a many yuletide celebration during my youth but none more fondly than the Christmas of 1940. The United States had yet to enter into World War II but the conflicts on the European continent and in Asia were being widely covered. The American media speculated that the U.S. was soon to enter the war. Occasionally, we would hear tidbits of adult conversation about the possible draft of able-bodied men into the military. But as for me and my younger brother and sister, the only thing we could think about that December was the upcoming Christmas.

Steady work was hard to come by, which meant that we were restricted to one article of clothing each and no toys. After a couple years of seasonal and handyman jobs, my dad secured a full-time job in the coal mines of West Virginia, with a decent wage. He and mom encouraged us to create a list of some of the items we wanted for Christmas from Santa. I was ten years old at the time and my brother and sister were seven and five, respectively. The three of us quickly complied, remembering the past two Christmases when Santa visited us only briefly. Excited with anticipation, I knew exactly what I wanted that Christmas in 1940. I made a point of saying so in a note to Santa:

PART 3: REFLECTIONS

"Dear Santa," I wrote, "The main thing I want for Christmas is a Roy Rodgers cap pistol. Just to be on the safe side," I added, "I would also appreciate any other toy you decide to leave."

I folded my note and told dad to make sure he gave it to Santa. Of course, by this time, I had already figured out that the Santa thing was pretty much a hoax and kept up a charade for the sake of my younger siblings. I knew my parents were not ready to deal with any expressions of disbelief from me.

Our community was surrounded by mountains with trees of all sizes. My brother and I found a small tree in the hilly woods, not too far from our house, sawed it off and towed it back to our home. Dad set the tree up and all family members joined in to decorate it. My siblings made long lists for Santa. They thought I was being odd for only asking for one specific toy. But I knew that if I received nothing else that one toy would satisfy me.

On that unusually restless Christmas Eve, I woke up, peeked out my bedroom door, only to discover mom and dad busily placing an assortment of packages under the tree. I jumped back into bed with no one the wiser of my quick peek-a-boo. The next thing I knew, I had fallen into a sound but contented sleep. I was awakened a few hours later by the

PART 3: REFLECTIONS

enthusiastic chatter of my siblings racing each other to check out the packages left by Santa under the tree.

I quickly followed and soon found presents with my name on them—a baseball mitt, a few games and some sweaters. Then came the box that, based on its obvious shape and size, could be nothing other than my Roy Rodgers cap pistol. There in all its splendor was a replica of the beautiful pearl handled pistol carried by Roy Rodgers in the movies, along with two rolls of caps. When I placed rolls into the cylinder of the pistol and pulled the trigger, it made a cracking sound that imitated the sound of a real gun. I was in seventh heaven.

At long last, I would no longer be the only person among my group of playmates without a cap pistol. The next time we gathered on the sandy weedy banks alongside the bluestone river to play war or cowboys and Indians, I would be able to participate. That Christmas night I went to bed with my cap pistol under my pillow thinking that maybe, just maybe, Santa Claus was real after all.

Thankfully, my youthful fancy for toy pistols did not morph into me becoming a second amendment fanatic against reasonable gun control measures. I have never nor do I anticipate buying or owning a real gun.

PART 3: REFLECTIONS

The Search for Freedom

As I reflect on the events that occurred in Charlottesville, Virginia on August 12, 2017, I am reminded of the *Live Free or Die* motto imprinted on the state of New Hampshire's license plates. It was the motto and clarion cry of the early colonists during their fight for freedom and independence from English control. It is also a motto that deeply resonates inside me whenever I think of the many years of slavery imposed upon my African ancestors, who were chained and shackled on these North American shores.

They may not have known the correct phrasing to describe the word freedom but there is no doubt in my mind that they yearned to be free of the treachery of slavery. In fact, Negro spirituals were born out of their yearning to be free. The lyrics to these songs closely followed the slave master's introduction of the Bible. A choice that proved fortuitous in not only providing a way of salvation for an enslaved people but also helped to fuel their hope for freedom. Their longing for freedom put them in the mind of Moses—a man who, under divine recourse, lead his Jewish brothers and sisters out of captivity in Egypt to a land promised to them by God. It was the inspiration behind the

PART 3: REFLECTIONS

famous words, "Go down, Moses, way down in Egypt's land. Tell old Pharaoh, let my people go."

When it comes to freedom today, I have mixed emotions because of my people's history in this country. I am grateful to live in a country that guarantees its citizens the freedom of speech, religion, free press and the right to peacefully assemble and protest. And yet, I am not blind to America's checkered past and its failings in upholding the constitutional rights and guarantees of all people. As an African American, I am cognizant of the segregation and second-class treatment of African-Americans, and how institutional racism has been allowed to flourish in this country, long after slavery was abolished.

The ongoing disputes over confederate statues and monuments, and the display of the confederate flag on public buildings, is evidence of the need to continue the fight for racial freedom. This is especially true when it comes to the forces that are hell bent on preventing African Americans from pursuing the American dream; that desire to keep them subordinate, unemployed, unable to vote and victims of unfair treatment by supposedly responsible law enforcement. Black communities overwhelmingly respect and desire law and order. The basic message of groups like *Black Lives Matter* is a call for mutual respect and the

PART 3: REFLECTIONS

uniformity of policing standards, and practices in the treatment of all suspects irrespective of their racial identity or ethnicity.

The axiom—innocent until proven guilty—has not always been followed in interactions between the police and people of color. The double standards impact the freedoms of all those who are subject to its mistreatment. The risk factor behind the DWB (driving while black) experience is not imaginary. There have been too many unwarranted stops of law abiding, unarmed black motorists (often ending with tragic results) to ignore this reality. It cannot be emphasized enough that African Americans do not seek, nor have they ever sought, any special privileges. They (we) simply want the same equal privileges afforded to other American citizens of different races, ethnicities and skin colors.

Freedom should be color blind. The fight for freedom and justice will continue until (as Martin Luther once put it) all God's children can say, *"Free at last, Free at last. Thank God almighty, we are free at last."*[3] In this worldwide quest for freedom, I still believe that love will inevitably triumph over hate and unity will eventually triumph over disunity

---

[3] Martin Luther King, Jr. *"I Have A Dream"* speech. Copyright 1963. Retrieved from https://www.archives.gov/files/press/exhibits/dream-speech

PART 3: REFLECTIONS

(despite the lack of moral leadership exhibited by our current President).

I believe that the common decency of American citizenship will one day reign supreme over the racial hatred and divisiveness of groups like the KKK, Nazi sympathizers and White supremacists. My optimism is fueled by the life of another historical figure—Nelson Mandela—who once said: *"No one is born hating another person because of the color of his skin or his background or his religion. People must learn to hate, and if they can learn to hate, they can be taught to love, for love comes more naturally to the human heart than its opposite."*[4] Question is how do we stop the condition of racism from becoming a learned behavior?

---

[4] Nelson Mandela. (1994). *"Long Walk to Freedom."* Retrieved from https://abcnews.go.com/International/ nelson-mandelas-inspirational-quotes/story?id=8879848

PART 3: REFLECTIONS

A New Paradise

It was a dark and moonless night. Adam and Eve were hiding behind a thick bush of vegetation, just outside a small midwestern town in the U.S.

Eve: "This is a strange land" she whispers to Adam, as she looks at all the people scurrying back and forth. "They have items all over their bodies."

Adam: "I think they call it clothing."

Eve: "Yeah, I guess they haven't heard of leaves or animal skin. It worked ok for us in the Garden of Eden."

Adam: "Yes, and we'd still be there if you hadn't eaten the forbidden fruit."

Eve: "There you go again blaming me for everything. I guess you've forgotten that you took a bite from the apple too."

Adam: "Ok, Eve, let's not argue about the past. What's done is done. We've got to figure out how to survive down here."

Eve: "Amen to that."

Adam: "Eve look over there! (A few yards to her right was a bin with the inscription, donated clothing).

Adam: "Some power must still be watching over us."

Eve: "God is good."

PART 3: REFLECTIONS

Adam: "All the time."

Adam: "I'll lift you up so you can crawl through the opening and see what it contains."

Eve: "Why can't I do the lifting? I'm nearly as strong as you are."

Adam: "Look at the size of the opening. I'm too big to squeeze through it."

The two of them proceed carefully through the bushes to the bin located at the end of an unoccupied parking lot. Adam lifts Eve up, allowing her to navigate through the small opening in the bin.

Eve: "There's plenty of what you call clothing in here! I think I've found some things that look like what people are wearing. Help me out."

Eve emerges from the bin holding an assortment of pants, dresses, shirts, skirts, blouses, under garments and shoes.

Adam: Great.

They quickly figure out which one should wear the pants and shirts and which one would wear the dresses, skirts and blouses; but they are puzzled when it comes to the under garments and shoes. They finally determine that since the under garments were smaller than the other items of clothing that they must go underneath. They came to a

PART 3: REFLECTIONS

similar decision about the shoes, discovering that some were too small for Adam and others too large for Eve. Now fully dressed, Eve stares at Adam:

Eve: "How do I look?

Adam: "You look different. How about me?"

Eve: "I'd say the same for you. I feel different. I'm not used to having clothes all over my body."

Adam: "Eve, do you feel what I feel?"

Eve: "What's that?"

Adam: "I feel a pain in my stomach. I'm hungry."

Eve: "Now that we are fully clothed, let's walk around and see if we can find something to eat."

Looking down the street, while cupping his hand over his eyebrows so he can focus better, Adam says:

Adam: "Look, there's a place that says food and shelter for the homeless."

Eve: "I guess that's us since we lost the one home, where we had everything. My stomach is telling me I'm hungry too."

Adam: "Well, let's give this place a try. I think we look presentable now."

Adam and Eve walk a short distance down the street, enter the shelter and are immediately greeted by a smiling man who ushers them to a table.

PART 3: REFLECTIONS

Smiling Man: "Welcome! We are serving baked chicken, string beans, mashed potatoes, chocolate cake and lemonade tonight. We'll bring your plate to you shortly. By the way, do you folks need shelter?

Adam and Eve both nod their heads, amazed at the stranger's hospitality.

Smiling man: "Fine. When you finish your meal, I'll show you to your room.

The smiling man departs. Adam looks around the hall watching people eagerly attacking their meal.

Adam: "Well the food sounds a bit strange, but the people around here seem to really enjoy it. Wonder what our lodging will look like?

Eve: "One step at a time, Adam. Let's take care of this strange food first, then worry about where we're sleeping."

The food arrives. Used to eating only fruits, nuts and raw vegetables, Adam and Eve are mesmerized by the strange aroma coming from the food as they gingerly pick up their fork and knife, imitating the other diners. After a few bites, Adam is both shocked and surprised:

Adam: "Hey, this is great tasting food. We never had anything like this back home in the garden."

PART 3: REFLECTIONS

Licking her tongue around her lips, Eve responds in kind:

Eve: "Yeah, I thought we had everything in the heaven we left. Maybe we're experiencing another type of heaven here on earth."

Adam: "That very well maybe but we'd better not get too complacent since I don't want to be kicked out of here too. We've got to find out what the rules are. I just overheard one of the diners ask a question about something called employment."

Eve: "What's that?"

Adam: "It is called work. I guess everybody down here is expected to work for their food, clothing and shelter. We can't just get free stuff every day. We were spoiled living in the garden, where being obedient was the only requirement to have our needs met. And we even managed to blow that."

Eve: "Don't remind me. What work will we do?"

Adam: "We'll find out soon enough. They call it earning a living. For now, let's just eat, sleep and be merry. We can't go back to the *Garden of Eden* and tomorrow is another day. So, we've got some learning to do."

Eve: "Yeah, I want to learn whatever rules there are."

Adam: "This time, would you please obey them."

PART 3: REFLECTIONS

Eve lets out a sigh of exasperation.

Eve: "Adam."

The two of them finish their food. The smiling man reappears to escort them to their room.

Adam: "Thanks for the hospitality. By the way, do you know where we can find jobs or what you call work?"

Smiling Man: "Down here, we take care of each other and we work very hard at it. Food and shelter are available for anyone at no cost."

Adam and Eve exchange puzzled looks.

Eve: "Maybe God is not angry with us after all. He could have sent us anywhere but He sent us to a place like this."

Adam nods in agreement.

Adam: "You know, I thought there was something strange about this place when I noticed its name: Paradise."

Eve smiles.

Eve: "Another paradise. How coincidental. We won't have any adjustment problems here. It'll be just like home."

Adam: "It will if you aim to please. Please remember to obey whatever rules there are, Eve."

Eve: "I will if you will."

And off the happy couple went.

PART 3: REFLECTIONS

Back Yards

Front yards are for public show
but if you really want to know

What makes a family go
to back yards, you must flow

That is where you will find
hints of activities that bind

Flotsam and Jetsum of a kind
that's reflective of the family mind

A tent, a swing, a barbecue pit
a rocking chair for someone to sit

A hammock, a swing and a stool
in addition to an above ground pool

It'll tell you much more
than the yard outside a family's front door

The backyard mirrors a family's focus
while the front yard is just hocus-pocus

To blend into a neighborhood similarity
leaving the back for family clarity

PART 3: REFLECTIONS

Believe or Not

It was a dark and stormy night. Periodic bolts of lightning illuminated the heavily wooded country side, accompanied by occasional bursts of thunder. Ruth and Harold were cozy inside their little cottage. A fire was burning brightly in the fireplace. Hot bowls of stew and a fresh loaf of bread were on the kitchen table, ready to be eaten. When the wind started blowing hard against the window panes and a loud crash of thunder boomed, all the lights in the cottage went out. Ruth hurried to light some candles, placing them on the table. Suddenly, there was a knock at the front door, followed by a voice.

"Help me. Please help me" the frail voice wept.

"Who in the world is out in this kind of weather," Harold muttered.

He walked towards the door guided only by the candle-lit room.

"Ask who it is before you open the door," Ruth warned.

Their cottage, which was located in the center of New York's Adirondack Mountains, was somewhat isolated. There was only one winding road that led from the closest town to their vacation community. This particular

PART 3: REFLECTIONS

night was their getaway from all the Halloween shenanigans they both deplored.

"Who's there? Who is it," Harold shouted.

"Let me in please," the female voice pleaded. "I've had an accident. My car veered off the road when I turned sharply to avoid hitting a deer. The car crashed into a tree, crumpling the right side. I need to call a tow truck."

Harold opened the door slightly, keeping the safety latch engaged.

"Don't you have a cell phone," he asked.

"Yes, but the battery is low and I can't seem to get any voice transmission. Mister, please help me. I'm damp and I'm cold."

The woman had stirred Harold's compassion. As he slowly unlatched the door to open it, Ruth looked on with a sense of growing apprehension. Standing there with rain water dripping from her hair and nostrils was a thinly built woman in her early to mid-twenties. Her facial features were dominated by large light blue eyes that seemed anchored on her face without any visible movement.

"Come on in," Ruth said. "I know you must be freezing."

The woman took several steps and then collapsed on the floor.

PART 3: REFLECTIONS

"Oh, my god," Ruth screamed. "She must have been hurt when her car hit the tree."

Ruth and Harold gently lifted their untimely visitor onto the living room sofa. Ruth removed the woman's soaking wet raincoat and spread a blanket over her. The woman's whole body stiffened as she bolted upright.

"Where am I," she said with her large eyes appearing even larger, as she gazed around the room.

"You're in our cottage," Ruth said. "My husband, Harold let you in after you knocked on our door. You said you were in a car accident. Shortly after you came in you collapsed on the floor before we got your name. By the way, who are you?"

"My name is Lucretia," the woman said. "Sorry if I inconvenienced you."

"What an unusual name," Ruth thought to herself.

"Were you hurt by the crash dear," Ruth inquired. "Perhaps we should call an ambulance for you and a tow truck for your car. Let me give you a cup of stew before you settle down to make your calls."

"I'm fine," Lucretia replied, eagerly slurping up the stew.

Lucretia looked sheepishly at her benefactors.

PART 3: REFLECTIONS

"I've got to tell you the truth, there was no deer and no car accident," she said.

Harold and Ruth exchanged perplexed glances.

"You see," Lucretia said, with her eyes and face glowing with a mischievous, half smirk of a smile, "You see, I'm a Halloween witch. I took some time off from the delightful experience of scaring kids just to be with you."

"Why us? We don't even believe in Halloween," Harold stammered.

"That's the reason I decided to pay you a visit," Lucretia said, as she floated off the couch and instantly disappeared through the closed door without opening it.

As soon as she left the room, the cottage lights immediately came back on and the storm quickly died down.

Harold and Ruth were speechless for minutes. Staring at each other, neither of them wanted to be the first to make a sound. In the eerie quiet of their cottage, they could hear each other breathing heavily. No longer able to contain himself, Harold blurted out:

"Do we have anything stronger than coffee! I don't believe what just happened and what we saw. If we tell our friends, they will think we are crazy! In fact, I'm not even sure that we are off our rockers," Harold said.

PART 3: REFLECTIONS

"Harold," Alice replied, snuggling in her husband's arms, "Our friends don't need to know. This experience is strictly between you and me. They can believe it or not."

PART 3: REFLECTIONS

Blame It On Aladdin

After a couple of years of on and off engagements, Sam and Beulah Johnson finally got married, on January 31, 2010, on a ranch called the *Hitching Post*, near San Diego, California. They were, respectively, 26 and 24 years old.

Theirs was a very small wedding with no more than 40 friends and family in attendance. They honeymooned for a week in Hawaii, waiting until they returned to open their wedding gifts. One of the gifts had no identification, identifying who it was from. As they carefully opened it, they were surprised to see that it contained a modern-day replica of the mythical Aladdin's lamp.

"It's a what," Sam asked of Beulah.

"It's Aladdin's lamp," she said, excitedly. "You know, the lamp with a genie in it that will grant you your heart's desire. All you have to do is rub it."

"That might have been true for the original lamp," Sam said, smiling. "But how many fake ones do you think are on the market now?"

Beulah didn't respond. Instead, she was deep in thought: "I wonder who could have sent this to us?" Turning to Sam, she said:

PART 3: REFLECTIONS

"Let's not do anything with the lamp until we find who gave it to us," she said, carefully placing it back into the box it originated from.

Over the next few weeks and months, their inquiries to friends and family provided no answers. They were at a loss for who or why someone would send the lamp to them anonymously. Until such time as the real owner could be identified, the lamp remained hidden away, packed in the box it had come in.

The two prominent chefs and lifelong residents of the *Eminent Restaurant* in San Diego, California, decided to seek employment on the East coast. Another chef and mutual friend in New York City recommended that they consider the internationally acclaimed *Windows On The World* restaurant located in the *World Trade Center,* who just so happened to be hiring chefs of their caliber and qualifications.

Several months after applying, Beulah and Sam received notification of their hiring and were told to report to work on September 11, 2001. Excited over their future prospect, they relocated to New York, acquiring a small apartment in Brooklyn which was only a short commute to the World Trade Center. The day before they were scheduled to report to work, they stumbled across the box containing

PART 3: REFLECTIONS

Aladdin's lamp, which ironically tumbling onto the floor from a larger box in the closet, as if to say, "Hey, remember me!" Beulah pulled the lamp out of the box, calling for Sam:

"Sam, I think this is a great omen for our new start," she said, rubbing the lamp's midsection.

"Genie, or whoever you are, keep us safe in this new chapter of our life," Beulah said.

"Woman, you're crazy," Sam said smiling.

"If the genie can keep us safe and make us successful at the fabulous *Windows On The World,* then I'm with you all the way." Sam said, amusingly, joining Beulah in stroking the lamp's midsection.

That next morning, while patiently waiting for their subway train which was running late, the World Trade Center Towers were struck and eventually collapsed. Of all the staff and customers in the North Tower on the 107th floor, where the *Windows On The World* restaurant was located, there were no survivors. Did Sam and Beulah believe their mysterious Aladdin's lamp had presented them with a good omen. Yes, they did indeed.

| PART 3: REFLECTIONS

Can Gerbils Do Arithmetic?

My ten-year-old daughter, Bridgette, tricked me. I finally gave in to her constant pleading, allowing her purchase two gerbils from the neighborhood pet store. She assured me that the gender of both were female, naming them Gertrude 1 and Gertrude 2. Quite honestly, they looked like Siamese twins to me. How she could tell the difference between the two, only my daughter and he siblings knew for sure. Not to be outdone, Bridgette and her siblings (one younger and older sister, and two younger brothers) claimed to have a similar differentiation ability. None of her siblings, however, were privy to what the clerk had told Bridgette—that while one gerbil was female, he was uncertain of the gender for the other. Like me, her siblings operated on the assumption that Gertrude 1 and 2 were both females.

Everyone was excited over the new additions to our family, except me. My idea of a family pet was limited to either a cat or dog. Nevertheless, we bought a covered cage for the gerbils, including an exercise gym with a wheel and activity ball. We filled the floor of the cage with wood shavings and old newspapers for their scratching delight; and their diet of sunflower seeds and water was scrupulously attended to.

PART 3: REFLECTIONS

The gerbils took to their new surroundings with great enthusiasm; and over the next few weeks, proved to be a source for family entertainment. Especially, for an old curmudgeon like me, as a somewhat resistant observer. To my uneducated eye, they were too close in resemblance to mice to ever be a pet that I would personally consider. But since the two brought so much joy and happiness to our family, I was glad to know that I had acceded to my daughter's wishes. Needless to say, this blissful spirit of contentment was completely shattered upon arriving home from work one day. The entire family had gathered in Bridgette's room, where the gerbils were located.

"What's going on," I inquired.

"Hi hon. I'll be right down," my wife responded, speaking through a slightly cracked door. I could hear murmurings of excitement coming from the room as someone asked, "What's dad going to say?"

"What's dad going to say about what," I hollered, curious as to what was going on inside the room.

Finally, my wife emerged from the room and came down stairs.

"Bridgette has something to tell you," she said.

"I think it would be better for you to go up to her room and talk to her."

PART 3: REFLECTIONS

My first thought was that one or both gerbils must have died, so I prepared myself to do some consoling.

"Dad, Gertrude had triplets," Bridgette gushed, as I opened the door to her room.

"Which Gertrude," I asked.

"Gertrude 1," Bridgette responded.

"Then Gertrude two must have the wrong name," I replied.

"I know dad," she said.

"I've already renamed him Heathcliff."

Bridgette then confessed that when we purchased Gertrude 2 in the store that the clerk had told her he was not certain of its gender. She had not bothered to tell me because she was afraid I would say no to the purchase.

Afterwards, my daughter and I made a pact: There would be no more gerbil purchases. Heathcliff, Gertrude and their offspring would be allowed to live out their natural lives. Of course, I never considered that this prolific duo would have three more little ones. The newborns did not last more than 48 hours. One night they were in the cage and the next day they were gone, obviously devoured by one or both of the parents.

After a couple years our household was gerbil free due to several accidents, old age and various complications.

PART 3: REFLECTIONS

The one subject that frequently comes up during family gatherings is the potential for a Guinness World Record, had the miraculous gerbil births been a product of two female gerbils. Although the gerbil's method of birth control was somewhat hideous, I would like to think that maybe, just maybe, Gertrude and Heathcliff could count. Perhaps, somehow, they knew that three offspring were enough and six was beyond their endurance.

PART 3: REFLECTIONS

Caribbean Odyssey

The setting is the early eighteen hundred, somewhere in the western Caribbean islands off the coasts of Aruba and Venezuela:

"We've been circling around in these waters for more than a month and our supplies are running low," muttered the captain of the pirate ship Jolly Roger, as it sat anchored some 20 miles off the Venezuelan coast.

His thoughts were suddenly interrupted by the excitable shouting of a grizzled sailor, who was posted as a lookout high up in one of the ship's central masts.

"Captain, a big one's coming toward us. From the direction she's coming from, I'd say she's probably loaded with cargo bound to Europe."

"All hands-on board," the captain quickly commanded.

As the scraggly but adventurous and loyal crew assembled on deck, the captain made an appealing promise:

"Men our days of rationing will soon be over. A big transport is approaching us and from the heading and direction she is coming, it looks like she is loaded with all kinds of goods for shipment, most likely headed to England.

PART 3: REFLECTIONS

There might be a few rich passengers on board, so guard your stations and prepared for attack."

The Jolly Roger moved briskly toward the incoming ship, unfurling its calling card—the cherished and feared pirate flag—brazenly advertising their presence. Gun crews readied their cannons. Any man who was not a gunner, carefully placed his sword or knife in his scabbard in anticipation of taking over the oncoming vessel.

The men of the Jolly Roger, who were mostly unlearned and unskilled from poor families, had two things in common: They loved being on the water and they easily took to the violent thuggery and pillage life of a pirate. Now, as the Jolly Roger got closer to its prey, the captain and crew became somewhat befuddled. The ship had no identifying markers, flags or visible cannon ports, as was common with cargo and passenger-carrying vessels.

"She has no big guns," the captain shouted, as the other vessel hoisted a white flag.

The crew of the Jolly Roger, itching for the excitement of a fight, groaned in disappointment. Peaceful takeovers were not exciting. Once the Jolly Roger came side-by-side with the other ship, the captain and a few select crew boarded the other vessel. What they witnessed gave them the shock of their lives. The vessel carried cargo, alright, but it

PART 3: REFLECTIONS

was human cargo. They had unknowingly and unwittingly intercepted a slave ship. On the deck and in the holds of the ship were approximately 100 men, women and children chain linked together by gender, many of which were in various stages of physical and mental stress.

Pirates were not known for their adherence to a strict moral code of conduct but the sights they saw sickened them. It was one thing to take over a ship, killing all who resisted them while relieving them of their possessions but quite another thing to aid in the support of inter-governmental trade and commerce. In their repugnance of all governmental authority, they transferred their animosity to the slave traders, not because they personally cared for the slaves as human beings but because they viewed the slave traders as extensions of the government they loathed. Why not seize the vessel, ridding the slave traders of their precious cargo? What concern was it of theirs if said cargo was human and being treated like cattle?

The captain had a decision to make. The Jolly Roger did not have the means to take on all the slaves on board, but they could capture the small crew in command of the slave ship with the expectation of making them pirates. The captain commanded his crew to board the slave ship to bind and transfer the ship's crew to the Jolly Roger. Either they

PART 3: REFLECTIONS

would become good pirates or suffer the consequence of being dropped off on some remote uninhabited island.

Several of the slaves understood English and had a basic knowledge of sailing. Upon hearing about their newfound liberation, they plotted amongst themselves to steer the ship on a course heading in the direction of Africa. After unshackling the slaves and dividing the spoils of ample supplies on board (fruits, grain, sugar, pork, coffee and the much-desired rum, which they kept for themselves), the Jolly Roger sailed off leaving the slaves to their own fate, to fend for themselves. Whether the slaves made it back to Africa or not during their quest is unknown. Whatever their fate, they were free.

Some years later, a ship was discovered anchored off an uninhabited island—a few hundred miles from where the earlier encounter between the Jolly Roger and the slave ship had taken place. A boarding party found a collection of human bones. Were they the remains of the slavers who encountered the Jolly Roger or were they the remains of the slaves? Herein lies the mystery of the Caribbean Odyssey.

PART 3: REFLECTIONS

Charles Russell: "A True Friend"

To me the word "friend" is not a word to be tossed around loosely. I certainly would not lump it into some anonymous, broad category of acquaintances, as so many people tend to do. The word *friend* has a special connotation. It epitomizes the height of trust, empathy, reliability, loyalty and honesty—all of which are essential elements of a true friendship but by no means is an exhaustive list of traits.

A true friend shares in your triumphs. He or she can be a voice of encouragement in addressing your challenges and disappointments; while at the same time being unafraid to acknowledge disapproval when warranted. A true friend recognizes human foibles and rather than dispense unmerited praise is unafraid to speak the truth.

Never in all of my life—outside my immediate family—have I ever met or found a more loyal and compatible friend than Charles "Charley" Russell. Charley and I shared the same last name but were not related as family. In the ten years we knew each other, we were in each other's life intermittently; meeting for the first time in the administration office of Duquesne University, a catholic liberal arts college in Pittsburgh.

PART 3: REFLECTIONS

We both were enrolling in college after the completion of our military service. Only a small number of Black students attended the college in those days and we naturally gravitated to tables in the cafeteria where we could have lunch together. It was in this setting that Charley and I got to know each other. We talked about our family backgrounds, our respective military service in the Army and Air Force, our academic and career interests and our relationships. I had met the girl who would eventually become my wife and Charley was just coming out of a broken relationship. We spent hours discussing a variety of topics, including the United States' race relations and what our perspective roles might be in making things better.

It was in the early 1950's, prior to the organizational efforts of Martin Luther King, Jr. There was a brewing national discourse among civil rights organizations to fight for more equal opportunities for African American citizens over a broad range of issues. Charley and I discovered that we had a lot in common, especially when it came to politics and our general outlook on life. He liked reading and writing as did I. We both enjoyed philosophy, debating and spectator sports. We also were two kindred spirits with similar tastes when it came to other social activities, including our preferences in food, music and humor.

PART 3: REFLECTIONS

The one big difference Charley and I is that he had wheels and I did not. One day, he cajoled me into going with him to meet a new girlfriend that he thought might be the one. I was not feeling any good vibes about it. It seemed apparent to me that while the girl was charming and polite, she was not really interested in Charley. I expressed my view when he pressed me to share my thoughts. Charley disagreed and said the girl was just shy upon meeting me for the first time. He had told her that I was his best friend. I hoped Charley was right about the girl. I was a bit more skeptical since he had a habit of falling for girls who were not really interested in him. By this time, I had introduced Charley to my future wife and asked him to be the best man at our wedding. He really took to La Verne, often telling me he wished he had met her first. Of course, I insisted that it would not have made any difference.

Charley agreed to be my best man. Shortly thereafter, he told me that he had broken up with the girl that he thought would be the future Mrs. Charles Russell. I felt bad for Charley and even tried to be an occasional matchmaker over his strident resistance. I got married at the beginning of my senior year when Charley was still a junior. During our first year of marriage Charley visited us frequently, sometimes with one of his latest lady friends and sometimes just solo.

PART 3: REFLECTIONS

He was there for the birth of our first child, driving us home from the hospital since I had not yet purchased a car.

When I moved to Washington, D.C. to accept a job in government, Charley was there to help us pack for the move. An only child, Charley loved telling people that we were "soul brothers" born to different parents. Not long after our move to D.C., Charley gave us some surprising news. He had decided to drop out of college during his senior year (the same college he had been attending only part time) to re-enlist in the army. I was supportive of his decision but shocked since I knew how much a college graduation meant to him. I suspected that he was the victim of another broken love affair but never admitted that this was the cause.

Charley loved to write. Over the next several years, as my family continued to grow, we kept in contact with each other, including a few visits when he was on military leave. Charley was eventually shipped to a base in California and the visits stopped but the letters continued albeit not as frequently as before.

I had not heard from Charley for some time, when I ran into a mutual former college acquaintance of ours who lived in Pittsburgh. This mutual acquaintance told me that he had heard that Charley's mother had died, which was confirmed a short time later in a letter from Charley himself.

PART 3: REFLECTIONS

He had also heard that Charley had met the girl of his dreams. I would receive only one more piece of correspondence from Charley, which came about six months later. He did not mention the girl of his dreams and gave no indication that he was dealing with any serious problems. My subsequent letters to him over the course of the next few months were returned, *Addressee Unknown – No Forwarding Address.*

All my efforts to track Charley down through the military and other sources were to no avail. Once his mother passed, he had no other relatives in Pittsburgh. Neither was there any documentation left behind concerning his last whereabouts. The only thing I found out is that he was involved in some type of military research project.

We knew each only for about ten years but Charley was by far, the closest friend I have ever had. We did not share the same parentage, but we were soul brothers long before the term was adopted by popular culture.

PART 3: REFLECTIONS

Chilly Grandma

Everyone should have a favorite grandma. Mine was Grandma Mandy. Grandma Mandy was a character, full of wit, with a great sense of humor. Standing exactly five feet tall and weighing barely 100 lbs., Grandma's facial features were quite attractive—even at her older age as she would often describe herself. She had a medium brown complexion, unusually thick eyebrows and long eyelashes which highlighted her most prominent feature, her large hazel colored eyes.

There was one aspect of grandma's nature that never changed. If the temperature was less than 80 degrees outside or more than 75 degrees inside, she was perpetually chilly regardless the season. Mom worried that grandma had thin blood or some other more serious problem, and constantly urged grandma to go for a medical checkup but Grandma Mandy obstinately refused. She had avoided doctors and most medicines her entire life. The only concession to her general ban on medications was to periodically take a dose of castor oil to clean out her system and to keep all her body parts operating correctly. She was disappointed throughout her life that she never convinced any of her five children or twelve grandchildren to join her in this regimen.

PART 3: REFLECTIONS

Most days, Grandma Mandy sat cheerfully in her favorite chair doling out advice on the issues of the day, regardless of whether that advice was sought or unsought. Of course, she did all of this while wearing one or two sweaters to keep out the chill—a chill that no one else in our household felt. As kids, we thought that grandma might be a little touched in the head, but we did not dare share our thoughts with our mother, who we knew would not appreciate hearing our opinions. When questioned why she felt chilly when everyone else was warm, Grandma Mandy would quickly remind us that she had never had a sick day in her life and still had all her teeth. Aside from her habitual use of castor oil, grandma attributed her good health and long life to the fact that she was always covered up against the chill. Afterwards, she would smugly end any conversation on the subject by pulling her sweater tightly against her chest.

Grandma Mandy died at the age of 92 in the manner she was accustomed to: Sitting in her rocking chair in a warm house with her sweater on. Her last spoken words to us were, "It's a little chilly today."

PART 3: REFLECTIONS

Coming Soon: "A New Holiday"

My assignment was to come up with a new holiday.

My idea of a great holiday would be procrastination.

A day strictly devoted to all procrastinators, active or potential.

I was going to write more about how it would be implemented.

Maybe someday I will.

But today, I have decided to procrastinate.

PART 3: REFLECTIONS

Conflicted

I was eating alone in a cozy, secluded corner at one of my favorite restaurants in Manhattan. When all of a sudden, I look up to see a couple (a man and woman), fashionably attired and coming in my direction.

"Oh God, they're going to rain on my privacy," I thought.

I liked the idea of having the corner to myself. The couple, who appeared to be in their early thirties, quickly selected the only other booth in the area, which sat directly in front of mine. The only saving grace for me was that the two booths were separated by a high partition shutting off any visibility between the two tables. I was extremely thankful for this because the last thing I felt in the mood for was some forced, convoluted conversation with complete strangers.

I had been hit by two major blows that day. The first was Sally, a long-term soul mate of mine, who decided to break up with me over my failure to make a serious commit towards marriage. The second my recent and unexpected unemployment due to downsizing from the advertising agency I worked for over a 10 year period. As I sat contemplating my present circumstances and foreseeable

PART 3: REFLECTIONS

future—both of which appeared somewhat bleak—I simply wanted to be alone with my fears and apprehensions.

Shortly after the couple sat down and had given the waiter their order, their casual conversation (although slightly muted) seemed to drift over to my unwelcomed ears. It was unnerving to say the least. I felt like a victim who had been duped by the FBI into ease dropping on their conversation, which at first, I tried to ignore, considering it of no business of mine. But certain phrases pricked my ears and demanded my attention, despite any desire on my part to remain indifferent:

THE PIMP: "Man, what about that client I set you up with last night. Was he the well-off dude I thought he was?"

THE PROSTITUTE: "He gave me double my asking price and said he wanted to see me again."

THE PIMP: "Did you set up another meeting?"

THE PROSTITUTE: "Yes, for tomorrow night. Same place, same time."

THE PIMP: "Did you get a look at his wallet, ID or anything personal?"

THE PROSTITUTE: "He's a business man from Buffalo here for a convention. His wallet was bulging with big bills and credit cards of every description. It was obvious he wasn't in the habit of entertaining prostitutes."

PART 3: REFLECTIONS

THE PIMP: "Why do you say that?"

THE PROSTITUTE: "He was very nervous and careless with the way he handled his money."

THE PIMP: "Well, he had to have big bucks to be staying at that hotel. Everything about him, from his attire to his physical appearance, shouted money. I saw him standing outside the hotel entrance looking around. You know I can spot a john at a distance. I walked right up to him and said, 'Man, you look like you lookin' for something. Maybe I can help you.' The look in his face told me all I needed to know. He was looking for some action and the rest is history."

THE PROSTITUTE: "What do we do next?"

THE PIMP: "First, keep the date, babe. I think we might hit it really big with this guy. Remember, I'll be in the room next door."

THE PROSTITUTE: "Ok, robbery is fine, but I don't want nothing else more serious than that happening."

THE PIMP: "Don't worry. We'll just take all the money he has on him and make a little visit to a few ATMs."

THE PROSTITUTE: "Ok but promise me no super rough stuff."

THE PIMP: "Babe, you know my word is my bond. As long as he cooperates all will go well."

PART 3: REFLECTIONS

THE PROSTITUTE: "What if he doesn't cooperate?"

THE PIMP: "Don't worry so much. Just turn your trick and leave everything to me."

After a few bites of food and some additional chit-chat, the couple paid their bill and left. They left me in a quandary of what to do. I didn't know who they were other than a pimp and his prostitute. No names were exchanged or used in their discourse with each other and neither did I know the identity of their intended victim. I reasoned within myself that I could call the cops but what good would that do? In a city the size of New York and with the paucity of information I had to convey, they would likely have no greater leads to go by than I did.

As I dealt with this new intrigue, it dawned on me that at least one positive thing had come out of the encounter: The fact that I could not help overhearing their conversation, followed by the fact that I could not get it out of my head, had relieved me of any excessive focus on my own problems.

As far as my personal problems were concerned, tomorrow was a new day. It would be a day of new possibilities that I could look forward to, with a great deal of hope. Secretly, I hoped that the pimp and prostitute's plans

PART 3: REFLECTIONS

would go awry. More importantly, I hoped that the prospective John might have a "come to Jesus moment" and after his night of adventure might forgo any future repeat rendezvous. I hoped he would shuffle his sweet little carcass back home to Buffalo.

PART 3: REFLECTIONS

The Joy of Competition—The Agony of Defeat

"Did they let you win?" the new kid in town asked with a degree of impertinence. I was, of course, insulted by the question. In my town, I was justifiably recognized as the king of checkers by my family, friends and casual acquaintances, who occasionally got together to play the game. The fateful day when my winning streak ended, occurred shortly after the kid challenged my capabilities, even after being duly informed of my title.

The kid said he played checkers only a little bit and wondered how soon we might engage each other. I quickly accepted the challenge, licking my lips at the prospect of another easy win. We agreed to meet the next day after school in the playground area where we generally gathered. I would bring my board and checkers. He would bring only himself. We would play a wide-open game—my favorite—allowing backward as well as forward jumps and giving maximum power to the king.

I made the first move and aggressively trying to best him with one of my reliable trap maneuvers. Instead, each move I made was co-opted by a counter move on his part that I had not anticipated. It was not long before the first game was over, then a second and finally a third before I had

PART 3: REFLECTIONS

enough. I went to shake the victor's hand but, being the competitor I was, I tried to give him a grip that he would long remember.

To my dismay, he out gripped me too.

PART 3: REFLECTIONS

Dinner for Two

La Verne generally got home from work an hour or so before I did. I was used to detecting aroma emanating from the kitchen as soon as I entered the house.

"What's for dinner," I asked, as I walked into the room.

"You must be kidding! Look around. Does it look like I'm cooking tonight?" she said.

We were a perfect match. After a year of marriage, the passion between us burned so brightly that we were romantically in sync. Plus, my wife loved to cook and I loved to eat her cooking. We had gone together for little over a year before getting married. During that time, we occasionally went on dinner dates about twice a month, sometimes pooling resources to pay for meals and at other times with me footing the whole bill. Now that we were married, I had forgotten about those intimate rendezvous.

Going out to a restaurant was the last thing on my mind. I was expecting to eat in but, as I walked into the kitchen, nothing edible was on the stove, in the oven or on the counter. I looked at my wife, suddenly realizing that I had forgotten our anniversary. Suddenly, a sharp pain grabbled my mid-section, as if I had absorbed a fist punch from Mike Tyson. With a guilt-ridden conscience, I looked into my wife's eyes and told a bold-faced lie:

"Happy anniversary honey. I left your card at the office. Where would you like to go for dinner?" I said.

"Anywhere you want to take me," she responded, "just so long as we go out."

"There is this new Polynesian restaurant that just opened up."

Stopping me mid-sentence, she said, "Russ, stop talking and let's just go."

I quickly freshened up and joined my wife downstairs, promising that would never ever forget our anniversary again. And the postscript to this story is, I never did.

PART 3: REFLECTIONS

Doing the Right Thing

Fifteen-year-old Samantha was usually easy going with a calm demeanor. She had an affable personality which changed only when she was called by her given name, Samantha, rather than her preferred nickname, Sam. At first acquaintance, she was quick to tell any and every one to call her Sam. Nearly everyone did except one noticeably obnoxious boy named Scotty. The two became acquainted as ninth graders on the first day of Social Studies class:

"I'll call you Samantha," he smirked, seeking to get her attention.

Taken somewhat by surprise, Sam retorted, "Then you won't get a response from me," purposing in her mind to avoid Scotty whenever possible. Sam, who was an excellent student and very popular among her peers, was excited about her first year of high school. Particularly, when it came to social studies class, which was taught by Miss Julia. Miss Julia had the reputation of being a no-nonsense teacher who ran a tightly controlled class room. Her tests were often very demanding and it was said that getting an "A" was comparable to running a marathon for the first time.

Unlike her peers who only took the class because it was required, Sam welcomed the challenge from Miss Julia.

PART 3: REFLECTIONS

As the ninth graders filed into the social studies room, Miss Julia stood at the door with pen and chart in hand, directing them to their assigned seats. Sam had just settled in her seat when she noticed that Scotty (aka Mr. Obnoxious) was coming her way.

"Oh God," she thought. "I hope he does not sit by me."

Unfortunately, Sam's hopeful thoughts were quickly diminished. Scotty plopped himself in the seat next to hers, staring directly at her.

"Hi, Samantha," he said, with a mischievous grin on his face.

Sam ignored Scotty's greeting, vowing to avoid eye contact with him at all cost.

"Maybe if I ignore him, he will finally get the message and leave me alone," she thought privately.

It was a common practice of Miss Julia to give her students a test on a weekly basis. The first couple of Fridays', when Miss Julia administered the tests, Sam remained vigilant in avoiding all eye contact with Scotty; and instead concentrated on her work, unaware of Scotty's prying eyes. By the end of the month she began to notice that Scotty had been copying off her work. Annoyed and upset over his blatant cheating, Sam wondered how she would

PART 3: REFLECTIONS

handle this. Weighing her options, she came up with five plausible solutions:

1. Tell the teacher and run the risk of being labeled a rat.
2. Stay quiet and try to cover her answers.
3. Confront Scotty about his cheating and ask him to stop.
4. Request a new seat assignment; or
5. Offer to work with Scotty in study hall to help him prepare for his tests.

After further consideration, Sam opted to give Scotty a chance at repentance; selecting option five while holding option one in reserve as a last resort. Sam had no illusions and was open to the possibility that this might not work. At the end of their next social studies class, Sam decided to approach Scotty. At first, he was surprised by her accusations, offering a weak denial. But when Sam told him that she knew he had been copying off her, he quickly became defensive:

"I'm not here to argue with you, Scotty. We both know you've been copying off me. I don't want to make trouble for you by reporting you to Miss Julia. Instead, I would like to help you," Sam said, in a non-threatening manner.

PART 3: REFLECTIONS

Somewhat bewildered that Sam did not turn him in, Scotty asked:

"How can you help me?"

"I know a little bit about studying and maybe I can help you organize your notes during study hall," Sam said.

Surprised by her generous offer, Scotty quickly decided to subside his hostility and come clean.

"Thanks for offering to help me Sam," he said sheepishly.

"I spend so much time making cheat notes that I never really take the time to study. I really don't like cheating, but I also don't want to fail this class." Scotty said.

"Wow, he finally called me Sam," Samantha reflected. "Maybe "Mr. Obnoxious" isn't so obnoxious after all."

"I'll see you at our next study hall," Sam said, smiling at Scotty.

For the first time, Sam saw Scotty in a different light. Study hall might prove to be quite interesting for the both of them.

PART 3: REFLECTIONS

Don't Call Me Polly

I'm still getting used to my life as a parrot.
How I got here, I do not actually remember.
What I do know is I woke up in this cage and some nut thinks he owns me.
I keep trying to tell him I do not belong here,
That I am a two-legged, two-armed human being like him but only smarter.

But for some reason, he does not take my comments seriously.
He breaks into laughter and wants to show me off to his friends.
If I had my arms and hands back, I would knock him on his fat behind.
He is at work now but before he left, he sprinkled some bird seeds in my cage.
  "I want steak, you idiot!"
He looks at me with a puzzled look on his face.
  "Wonder where he learned that from?"
If I was back in my human body, I would tell him his mother taught me.

PART 3: REFLECTIONS

But that response would probably be over the nit-wit's head.

So, I just stare at him, mimicking the same dumb clueless look he gives me.

I then decide to conjure up a lie:

"I escaped from the cage my previous owner kept me in.
He left a piece of steak on his plate.
I nibbled on it and I have been hooked ever since.
If you are going to keep me happy and talkative,
then you better get some steak in this cage!"

Soon, he is on the phone, talking to a friend:

"Joe, you are not going to believe this!
I've got a parrot and he's demanding that I feed him a steak."

I could not hear Joe's response but Bozo—I mean my temporary owner until I can
get back into my human form—was in my face again.

"Ok, I'll bring you some steak when I return from work.
But you better be good."

By "being good," I knew this "a-hole" meant he wanted me to talk until I got hoarse.

"Up yours!"

PART 3: REFLECTIONS

Finally, he is gone.

I looked at myself in the hall mirror.

I am handsome, almost regal, with green and red feathers.

Well, I guess if am forced to be a parrot, might as well be a good looking one!

Uh oh, feeling hunger pains.

I look around my cage and see the bird seeds scattered on the floor.

I use my beak to pick up a few and, to my surprise, they are not half bad.

> *"They'll make a great appetizer to go along with my steak!"*

Maybe life as a parrot can be endured.

If only Bozo can remember one rule: Never ever call me Polly!

PART 3: REFLECTIONS

Down with Akrasia

My youngest daughter gave me an exercise chair once that was equipped with all sorts of tension belts and pulleys, for stretching the legs and arms and strengthening the shoulders. She went on to point out to me that the chair came with a book of pictorial diagrams of more than two dozen exercises.

"It'll be great for your arthritis dad," she said, as she proceeded to assemble the chair.

Both my daughter and I was excited, and I could not wait to get into the chair. For the first month or so, the chair and I had daily acquaintance of 15 to 30-minute sessions. Suddenly, something inexplicable occurred in that I missed a session. My initial exercise fervor had waned. Why? Because it became clear to me that while I was regularly exercising my arms and legs, the lack of instant gratification was evident.

"No pain, no gain," my daughter insisted.

I discovered, to my dismay, that one missed session could easily morph into more missed sessions. Over the succeeding months, my relationship with the chair became less and less frequent, as I found myself finding excuse after excuse to put it off. Not only had I let my daughter down but

PART 3: REFLECTIONS

I had, more importantly, let myself down. I felt guilty, really guilty.

A quick trip to our town library helped me better understand my lack of enthusiasm and follow through. The fault it seemed lie in something called *akrasia,* which instantly made me feel better. What is akrasia you ask? Well, according to an article on in *Discover Magazine,*[5] the word was coined centuries ago by Greek philosophers to define "a state of acting against one's better judgment." A less benign description could be described as "a weakness of will."

Akrasia, according to the article, is not a matter of "personal failing, but [rather, the] result of a cognitive bias that strikes us all." It relates more to "time inconsistency" and the "tendency to discount the future in favor of the present." There is this tendency on our parts then, to splurge on things in the present that are desired but not needed. A good example of this is the difference between spending money that is earned on personal pleasures versus investing said money into a savings plan that will benefit us long term.

Our brains, it would seem, has competing systems that are often at war with each other. The compulsive system focuses on the here and now. For example, me thinking of all the other things I could be doing instead of exercising, without factoring in the benefit of what exercise will

PART 3: REFLECTIONS

accomplish for me in the long term. Armed with this new information, I now understand the significance of having the patience to get back to exercising and sticking with it daily, to derive its long-term benefits. Patience is in. Akrasia is out.

PART 3: REFLECTIONS

Family Matters Matter

A counselor once told me that sometimes family issues are among the most intractable issues to resolve. Case in point, Russ received a call from his wife, Ellen, just as he was preparing to leave from work:

"Honey don't forget to pick up a five-pound bag of apples from *Stop and Shop* on your way home and make sure you get the ones that are labeled freshly picked," Ellen said.

"Why not just any five pounds of apples," Russ asked.

"Because the insert from the newspaper had a picture of the five-pound bag of apples with the label 'freshly picked' on sale," she retorted.

"Why all the questions? You act as though I asked you to get something unusually exotic and hard to find," she said.

"Oh, I was just wondering about your emphasis on freshly picked," he said.

"Well, since you asked, another reason I wanted the freshly picked apples is because mature apples picked right off the vine make the best pies. When I accepted Aunt Sophia's wedding invitation she asked if I would bake

PART 3: REFLECTIONS

several apple pies for the small reception following the nuptials," Ellen responded.

"Ok already. I'll get the apples you want," Russ hastily agreed.

"I don't know why Sophia can't do a quiet 'I do' with only her and the prospective groom present. After all, this is her fourth walk down the matrimonial aisle and she is (as the expression goes) no spring chicken!" Russ said.

"That's not very nice Russ. Sometimes you can be so unromantic, even cruel, that I wonder what we have in common," Ellen reprimanded.

"Well, the one thing we definitely don't have in common is your affection for Aunt Sophia. One would think she was your blood relative and not mine," Russ retorted.

"She's always been nice to me and to you too. You've just got this vendetta against her that you can't drop," Ellen said.

I admit, I should have let the whole matter drop then and there but I was driven to add this rejoinder:

"All the nice in the world can't make me forget what she did. Talking about cruel, her cajoling my late mother for possession of our family heirloom—a full-length picture on canvas of my great grandfather in his World War I uniform

PART 3: REFLECTIONS

as a Calvary officer—takes the prize for being cruel," Russ said.

"Russ, in case you have forgotten, your mother was Sophia's sister. How many times must Sophia retell the story of how, before your mother's passing, she asked Sophia to take custody of the picture?"

"I just don't believe her," I stubbornly replied.

"My mother knew how much I cared about that rendering of my great granddad. I know she would have wanted me to have it." Russ grunted.

"You act as if Sophia has packed the picture away from view. It's hanging on the wall in her den for anyone to see." Ellen barked.

"I know, but I just think it should be in our den and not Sophia's. I am fully aware that Sophia is not going to give up her possession of the family heirloom, but I will always feel as though I should be the rightful owner," Russ lamented.

I do not think I will ever convince my wife of my position. As I stated at the start of this little opus, some family problems are indeed intractable.

PART 3: REFLECTIONS

Freedom

In my humble opinion, George Orwell's quote, *"freedom is the right to tell people what they do not want to hear,"* is valid but only up to a point. The point at which it is not so valid is when the telling or conveyance of truth becomes unnecessarily hurtful to another person. Free speech has its limits and does not come without a price. While I agree that in a free and open society we should be able to state views and take positions that may not be consistent with the opinions of many (or most people), this should not be done in a way that could potentially threatens public safety and security.

This is exactly why there is a permit process for public rallies, marches and speeches. A *civil* society permits the expression of unpopular opinions but sets standards on how, when and where such sentiments can be expressed in public. For example, consider the constraints placed on our writing group in voluntarily writing about subject matters relating to religion and politics. Why do we do this?

We do it, presumably because we assume there will be varying views and do not want to risk that someone could be hurt or annoyed by someone else's views on a given subject. While I may not be in full agreement with this

PART 3: REFLECTIONS

prohibition, I completely understand it. On the other hand, if we went full throttle with the Orwellian concept of 'telling it like it is, whatever the circumstance,' I fear society would be even more fractured and fragmented than it is today.

PART 3: REFLECTIONS

Green

There is something about the color

GREEN

that stands out among all others I've seen

To me it represents the essence of

LIFE

the rich leaves of majestic trees

on branches that pierce the air like a knife

Reaching out and all around

over the lush green of plants and flowers that

ABOUND

Green has a special look and smell among all other colors

IF LIFE HAD A COLOR

WHAT ELSE COULD IT BE BUT GREEN?

PART 3: REFLECTIONS

Henry Jeffries

Seventeen-year-old Henry ("Hank") Jeffries was the spark plug and *Energizer Bunny* of any group he was part of. All of his jokes and personal antics were original and seemingly never ending. Those who knew him thought that he was surely destined to be a comedian one day, making millions of dollars.

A roly-poly kind of guy, Hank stood about 5'9" inches tall and everything about him was round. He had a round barrel-chested body and a round face which was dominated by a set of large round brown eyes—eyes that seemed to illuminate the tan coloring of his skin. The son of a Vietnamese war bride and an African American soldier, Hank's racial mixture was frequently the center of parodies he constructed about himself. Hank was always on, always up and always flying high. One of his closest friends would often say, *"I can say with almost absolute assurance that the one word that none of us would have ever used to describe Hank is conflicted."*

When I first deliberated over this writing assignment, I immediately thought of conflict in its larger context: Nation against nation. One religion against another. Hostilities based on ethnic differences. Historic conflicts of epic

PART 3: REFLECTIONS

proportions. As I began to think more intrinsically about it, I realized that the writing assignment has more to do with an exploration of complexities: Likes vs. dislikes. Wants vs. desires. Fears vs. apprehensions. You know, all the things that make us tick—things that can and often do serve as a breeding ground for the internal conflict we deal with personally or through the personalities of characters we create. In my conclusion of it all, I was reminded of Hank Jeffries.

It was a typical high school Friday evening before a long weekend. Monday was Memorial Day and school would be out. Hank's class had a first period study hall but something was missing. There was no Hank. Notes were passed back and forth:

Has anyone heard from Hank?

Wonder if he sick?

Did his family go out of town?"

Speculation continued until Alice burst into the room, late as usual, with the usual permission slip. She asked the teacher if she could make an announcement to the class.

"For those of you who may be wondering where Hank is this morning," she began, "his mother called my mom and said that he is in the emergency room at the community hospital. I don't know what his condition is or

PART 3: REFLECTIONS

what happened. All I know is his mom called just as I was rushing out the door to catch the school bus."

A collective pall settled over the classroom. Anyone who knew Hank, knew that something unusual must have happened. Hank never missed a day of school. While not everyone was part of his coveted "best friend's" list, no one disliked him. The fact that no one knew what his condition was or why he was in the hospital, quickly became rife for speculation—a speculation that lasted throughout the remainder of the school day.

Alicia was particularly struck by the news about Hank. She had been the last student to speak to him yesterday as he got off the bus, they jointly rode together each day. Hank had asked Alicia if she would accompany him to the senior class dance. Alicia had responded, as gently as possible, that she had a date, offering to pass off one of her girlfriends as a possible substitute. Of course, Hank had no intentions of pursuing Alicia's suggestion. Instead, he just smiled as he hopped off the bus:

"I'll be back again and again until one day you say yes, Alicia."

Alicia smiled back, believing that Hank had accepted her "no" quite well. Alicia (like everyone else in the classroom) found Hank fun to be around; but she had no

PART 3: REFLECTIONS

serious interest in pursuing a dating relationship with him. Hank's thoughts about Alicia, on the other hand, were quite different. He was conflicted in that he had fallen in love with Alicia, without knowing exactly when or how it had happened. Maybe it was the way Alicia crinkled her nose or the way she parted her lips when he told one of his jokes. Whatever it was, he felt a chemistry with Alicia and he was certain she shared a similar chemistry with him.

After dinner, Hank had retired early to his room to watch one of his favorite sitcoms on television, before falling asleep. He had been musing over a routine he was planning to test out on his classmates and wondering how Alicia would handle it. Slipping in and out of consciousness, Hank hears voices:

"It's good you got to him as soon as you did, Mrs. Jeffries," the attending physician in the emergency room said.

"He'll have some lingering soreness in his neck and chest for a day or two. We'll keep him sedated and under close observation. Here is a list of referrals for psychiatric counseling when he is discharged."

"I must be in a hospital," Hank thought, as he slowly began to remember the activities of that night.

PART 3: REFLECTIONS

When he got up to get ready for school, Hank was thinking about how deeply Alicia's rejection had hurt him. Purely as an experiment, he had thrown a blanket over the beam in his bedroom, stepped onto a chair and tied the end of it into a knot around his neck. He had not meant to kick the chair from under his feet but had somehow lost his balance. Now, he was in the emergency room and this was no laughing matter.

Hank began to worry—not about his physical or mental condition but about his classmates. Especially, Alicia.

Would he ever be able to make them laugh again?

How else could he get their attention?

Hank's internal conflict went well beyond Alicia. He did not feel good about himself. In his mind, he was not smart enough or handsome enough to be a winner in life. So, he created a caricature that both he and his friends could laugh at and with. The only problem is, the caricature of a funny man that he had become did not allow him to be who he really was. In the end, *"Make them laugh,"* became his epitaph.

PART 3: REFLECTIONS

How Much Can One Friend Bear?

The saying, "Two's company, three's a crowd," did not apply when it came to my two best friends, Doris and Ralph. We were so close that we jokingly called each other brother and sister, even though there were no formal family ties between us. We had our own little posse all through high school; and when the three of us enrolled in the college of our choice, we remained close.

Our bond was forged during Junior High School as new Freshmen seated alongside each other during our English, Science and Math classes. Through casual conversation, we slowly discovered that the three of us—two guys and one girl—had a lot in common, including our mutual sense of humor and observation of people and life in general. Before we knew it, we became bosom buddies. We attended sports games, parties and movies together. The only time we were not together was during formal events like the prom, where we brought some non-serious date of the opposite gender. Even then, to the consternation of our dates, we would spend more time chit chatting with each other than with our dating partner.

As best I can recall, things began to change shortly after the start of our Sophomore year. It started with small

PART 3: REFLECTIONS

inconsequential things. In the past, Doris was always positioned between Ralph and me, whenever we walked to various destinations on campus. At some point, Doris started walking flank to his outside. Periodically, I would observe them holding hands and concentrating on each other, seemingly oblivious to my presence.

"Hey guys? What's up?" I would yell out.

My intentional inquisitiveness always paid off for a brief second and we would become a threesome again. After a while, I began to feel like a fifth wheel on a four-wheel vehicle. The on again off again type of inclusion and exclusion went on for months, which made me feel increasingly like I had involuntarily volunteered to participate in a threesome relationship. Inevitably, this resulted in a bit of tension between us:

"Russ, I've got something to tell you," Ralph finally shared.

"I think I know already, Ralph." I responded.

"It's about me and Doris. We've discovered that we have strong feelings for each other. I don't know how it happened, but I no longer see her as my sister, and she no longer sees me as her brother."

"Yeah, so I've observed," I said.

PART 3: REFLECTIONS

"Neither Doris nor I want you to feel left out. You're still our best friend," Ralph said.

"Are you sure about that Ralph? Does Doris even know you're talking to me about this?"

"She certainly does," Ralph snapped. "In fact, she asked me to talk to you first before she discusses it with you."

"It would be nice to hear from her," I said.

Later that same day Doris called:

"Russ, Ralph told me that you and he talked. I just want you to know that our relationship grew before we even knew what direction it was headed. I want you to know one thing, Russ. You are still the best friend either of us have ever had or known. Neither of us would ever want to do anything to hurt you. And we certainly don't want to lose your friendship or break up our group. We didn't set out to fall in love. It just happened."

"Love you say? So, tell me one thing Doris. Are you sure it's really love you have for each other?" I asked.

"Russ, we're really committed to each other. Someday we hope to get married and have you as our best man. Ralph wanted me to make sure that you knew that" Doris said.

PART 3: REFLECTIONS

"Thank you, Doris. Why didn't Ralph tell me that himself. I only wish happiness for the both of you," I had responded.

"I guess I'll be talking to Ralph again sometime soon."

Several weeks later, another subtly occurred. During our Spring break from college, Doris went home to work at her part time job while Ralph and I (our relationship was mended after a frank discussion that cleared the air), remained on campus for two-week baseball tryouts. The two of us were housed in one of the school's two co-ed dorms. During one particularly tough training day, I twisted my ankle after fielding a ground ball and decided to retire early with the coaches' permission.

As I laid in my bed with my leg elevated and an ice pack on my swollen ankle, I suddenly heard voices outside a nearby window. Curious, I peeked out the window to only witness a scene that I had not expected to see. A man and a woman were in a close embrace, passionately kissing one another. The woman's face was turned towards me and I recognized her as a member of the cheerleading squad that was practicing on a field near our baseball camp. As I looked more closely—to my surprise—I noticed that her kissing partner was none other than my very close and dear friend, Ralph.

They were really getting into it. As I backed away from the window, I concluded that this was not a platonic "peck on the cheek" type of relationship. I immediately thought of Doris and felt sorry for her. I was not sure what I felt about Ralph. Thoughts of infidelity coursed through my mind. What should I do? Should I confront Ralph, tell Doris or say nothing. I finally decide that the best course of action was to just sleep on it. I was not certain if or when I would talk to Ralph to let him know what I saw.

Then again, what about Doris? Telling her did not feel right to me. Perhaps it was best that she find out for herself about Ralph's "so-called" confirmed commitment. Hopefully, sooner rather than later, she will find out. The only certainty for me is that I knew that our longstanding threesome was no more.

PART 3: REFLECTIONS

Seeing Is Not Always Believing

Sometimes, what you see is not always what it is. Take for instance, Tom and Nancy Gray. Both were retired and in their mid-sixties. They had moved into a senior living community in 1965, shortly after their retirement. Almost instantly, they were recognized for their cheerful outgoing personalities and the deep affection they displayed for each other whenever they were in public. They soon became known as the "love birds," an appellation they happened not to mind at all.

One early Fall day, about six months after the Grays' had moved in, the neighborhood's busybody, Mrs. Jones (who just so happened to be the closest neighbor in proximity to them), saw something strange going on at the Gray residence. Underwear was being tossed onto the lawn from one of the upstairs bedroom windows. Intrigued, she gazed a little longer from her observation post in the corner of a large picture window. To her surprise, miscellaneous articles of male clothing followed the same flight path as the underwear. The party finally ended with the toss of an empty suitcase. Shocked by all of the shenanigans, Mrs. Jones heard a female voice shouting in a belligerent tone:

"If I could, I would throw you out the window too!"

PART 3: REFLECTIONS

Surely, this was not the loving Mrs. Gray who always spoke in a soft, ladylike manner. As she digested the thought, Mrs. Jones heard the somewhat muffled voice of a man that she took to be Mr. Gray:

"Honey, you don't understand. I can explain."

What immediately followed was a rash of expletives from Mrs. Gray, concerning Mr. Gray's numerous marital indiscretions. The language coming out of Mrs. Gray's mouth was too purple for Mrs. Jones' modest and delicate ears and yet, too mesmerizing to stop her from listening. Finally, with the recollection and recital of past misdeeds now apparently over, Mrs. Jones turned her face more fully toward the Gray residence. She was startled to discover to see another face staring directly at her. It was Mrs. Gray standing before her open bedroom window and she was not smiling. The neighborhood busybody had been caught red-handed in her snooping but what a sight she had seen and what language she had heard. As Mrs. Jones slinked away from her window. She could not get to her phone quick enough:

"Love birds huh," she hissed, "sometimes what you see is not what it really is."

PART 3: REFLECTIONS

Lost

It was almost midnight and my wife, La Verne, was not home. I tried not worrying but could not help remembering the last time she was late. It was five years ago. As I mentally dredged up the past, I could not help but see similarities between then and now. In both instances, as Vice President of Communications for her company, La Verne had attended a late-night meeting with the Board of Directors at their corporate headquarters in downtown Seattle. Normally a half hour drive from home, she had not contacted me to explain her lateness. Around 2:00 a.m. in the morning, I had received a call. Feverish with anxiety and worry, I picked up the phone and noticed it was from an unknown number.

"Russ, I'm ok. I misplaced my cell phone and could not call you. A repairman from AAA is allowing me use his phone," she had said.

"Triple A? Were you in an accident?" I asked.

"Not exactly," she said.

La Verne proceeded to give me the short version of a long story: Apparently, shortly after the board meeting had ended around 9:00 p.m., she found herself in an unusual predicament. On her drive home, she ran into a major

PART 3: REFLECTIONS

accident on the highway and the police had set up a detour. Unfamiliar with the roads in this heavily wooded, sparsely settled area, she had wandered off her intended route and gotten lost. When she pulled over to the side of the road to call home she discovered that her cell phone was missing. She drove around for a while, trying to find her way back to the main roads but found herself riding around in circles. Suddenly, she hears a thumping sound. She had hit something in the road, causing a flat tire.

Her heart now racing, with all kinds of fears percolating in her mind, she took the best course of action: She pulled over to the side of the road, locked herself inside the car and turned the car's emergency flashers on. Keenly aware that not every passerby would have the best intentions, she prayed that a law enforcement officer would eventually pass by. After waiting nearly an hour, she saw in her rear-view mirror what appeared to be the dome of a police cruiser approaching her location. The officer pulled up and motioned for her to roll down her driver's side window.

She happily explained to the officer that she was lost and had a flat tire. He in turn called AAA, provided her with directions on how to get back on the road that would take her home and conveniently stayed with her until the AAA

PART 3: REFLECTIONS

repairman arrived. The experience proved to be traumatizing for both me and my wife, despite the happy ending.

"Could this really be happening again?" I asked myself.

My thoughts now unfocused, I had this overwhelming sense that I was being lifted and transported somewhere distant. I heard my name being called by a voice that sounded like my wife:

"Russ! Russ!" she yelled.

I could feel hands tugging at my arms and clasping my hands.

"Russ!" La Verne called out again.

I struggled to open my eyes.

"Is that you La Verne? When did you get home?" I asked.

"I've been home dear. I've been here with you in the hospital for the past five days."

With great effort I forced my eyes open and looked around.

"This is a hospital. I'm in a hospital bed. Why am I here?" I asked.

"You had a fall dear. You fractured your skull and you had severe swelling on the brain. We thought we were going to lose you but everything is ok now. The doctors

PART 3: REFLECTIONS

assured me that you are going to be fine and there is no permanent damage." La Verne said.

"But what about your board meeting? You were late returning home and you never called. How did you get home?" I asked, inquisitively.

"I haven't been to a board meeting in five years, Russ," she said.

"The doctors and nurses on their daily rounds heard you murmuring periodically about a board meeting. But they attributed it to the blow you received when you fell. Somehow, and we do not know how exactly, the force of the fall created a residual cognitive memory of an event that happened five years ago. I knew the experience of me getting lost was traumatic for me but I did not realize how upsetting it was for you."

Still trying to process everything, I pulled La Verne close to me:

"I love you, La Verne."

"I know you do dear. I love you too but promise me, no more falls please. We don't need that type of excitement in our lives," she said.

PART 3: REFLECTIONS

Nick Names and Pain

His name was James Henry. But for some reason, he had been saddled with the nickname, Ham Brain. I do not know exactly when or how he obtained the nickname or who the classmate was who originally coined it. What I do know is he was an average student of average intelligence. He did not have any odd or peculiar physical features, like an abnormally large head to warrant the nickname. If he had, then perhaps the unkind gesture in nicknaming him would have been justified, given the nature of some students who like to overemphasize other people's flaws.

I simply recall how in the fourth grade most of our fellow classmates rarely called him by his given name—leaving that practice solely to our teacher. Among all our class mates only Lucy Jones and I addressed him as James; which gave him a welcomed reprieve from the incessant name calling. He was forever grateful for our small act of kindness and, in turn, eventually became a close friend.

Of course, we suffered some ostracism for refusing to go along with the pack. Both Lucy and I had a strong sense of fair play in that we were both very opinionated and not at all reluctant to defend ourselves from those who chose to call him Ham Brain. We thought they were unusually mean to

PART 3: REFLECTIONS

James, for no reason. In the end, we were unsuccessful in shaming them out of their persistent name calling, while still maintaining our ongoing friendship with James.

By the time high school graduation rolled around, many classmates had grown out of the incessant name calling; but there were still a few who persisted in taunting him. James had developed an exceptionally thick skin by that time and routinely put his tormentors in their place, returning more vitriol than either Lucy or I could have ever dished out. After graduation, I lost touch with both James and Lucy.

Whenever I think of those days—how Lucy and I were sympathetic in our loyalty towards James—it reminds me of an earlier occasion my life. I was also a victim of name calling by a former classmate who nicknamed me Jug Head after beating him at marbles on numerous occasions. The classmate eventually moved and thankfully, the nickname did not stick. When it came to James, I had no other choice but to align myself with him because I understood exactly how he felt.

PART 3: REFLECTIONS

Patriotism

Fidelity, love and loyalty are the building blocks of patriotism. However, being patriotic does not require blind love or blind loyalty.

We are not perfect. No nation is. We can recognize our shortcomings while still personifying the American dream of personal freedom and equality for all. To affirm our patriotism should not be done at the cost of a denial of our imperfections. Freedom of speech, freedom of the press and freedom of assembly are the bedrock of democracy. But I would argue that it is the freedom of dissent that serves as the life sustaining fiber of patriotism.

Hanging out the American flag on July 4 is a wonderful patriotic act. But having the wit to move beyond symbolization—to decently treat each other with respect on a daily basis, promoting sisterhood and brotherhood while working to build a more egalitarian society, is how we live out the American dream. This is a dream that truly makes us unique as a nation. In the final analysis—as President John F. Kennedy stated during his Inaugural Address in Washington, D.C. on January 20, 1961—it is not what our country can do for us but what we can do for our country that really counts:

PART 3: REFLECTIONS

"And so, my fellow Americans, ask not what your country can do for you; ask what you can do for your country. My fellow citizens of the world ask not what America will do for you, but what, together, we can do for the freedom of man."[5]

In my opinion, the commitment of a shared sacrifice between us all is what loving country and true patriotism is all about.

---

[5] The Guardian. (2007, Apr. 22). *Great Speeches of the 20th Century: John F. Kennedy.* Retrieved from https://www.theguardian.com/theguardian/2007/apr/22/greatspeeches

PART 3: REFLECTIONS

Presumptions Can Lead to Assumptions

Presumptions can easily lead to assumptions and, in the end, both can be wrong. I learned this invaluable lesson through my encounter with a girl named Eunice. I remember Eunice well, not only because we both were in the ninth grade but also because of the singular event that brought us together.

Arm wrestling was a popular fad back in the day and one that most girls regarded as an "all-male" activity. Among the relatively few girls who participated in the sport, Eunice had acquired the reputation of being one of the strongest girls in the school. I had a similar reputation among the boys that I was also extremely proud of.

I never viewed Eunice as a serious competitor because she was, after all, just a girl. Plus, she was not in any of my classes. She may have been unusually strong for a girl, but her strength could not match my cocksure attitude as a boy. In the final analysis, boys are stronger than girls or, at least in my mind, they are supposed to be. By the time the two of us entered Junior High, Eunice's exploits had grown considerably. So much so, that there were occasional whisperings and wonderment about her actual gender.

PART 3: REFLECTIONS

As she continued to mature, Eunice began to exhibit all the features of a sixteen-year old girl growing into womanhood. Not more than 5'2" tall, Eunice was compact and curvaceously built. She was every inch a female and extremely attractive, with large light brown eyes dominating a dark-skinned, oval-shaped face. On the days when she was not sparring with some hapless challenger, her nails were perfectly polished and manicured. In my mind, Eunice was strong but not as strong as I was. She was a girl and I was a boy—a distinction that I made note of after watching most, if not all, of her matches.

However, in the Spring of my ninth-grade year, this boy (who was relatively new to the school and someone I had just defeated in an arm wrestling challenge) made an off-cut remark that caught me off guard:

"I bet you can't beat Eunice," he said.

"What do you mean?" I replied.

"You know that Eunice is a girl, right?" he responded.

"I had a match with her last week when nobody was around, and she beat me. I bet she's stronger than you too," he said.

Had I known the meaning of the word "stronger" at the time, I would have told the kid his comment was

PART 3: REFLECTIONS

preposterous. Instead, the only words that came out of my mouth was that he was crazy and a sore loser. Eventually, word got out that I was afraid to arm wrestle Eunice. I did not like it one bit and was fed up with the slanderous effort to tarnish my reputation. Now, mind you, Eunice and I were not personal enemies. We always spoke warmly to each other whenever our paths crossed. But at this stage of the game, my personal pride was a motivator. When the opportunity arose in our exchange of classes, I would propose the one challenge that neither of us had ever broached to each other before:

"Eunice, would you like to arm wrestle me?" I asked.

Eunice seemed genuinely startled by the question, but her eyes lit up.

"I don't care. It's alright with me," she said smiling.

I was a bit taken back by her answer because I had always imagined that she would say no. Especially considering how, in the final analysis, I would likely win since I was a boy and she was just a girl. We set a date for our contest to take place the following Friday after the end of our last class.

On that Friday, Eunice and I sat down in two facing chairs, across a desk, with our own respective posse's huddled nearby. It has been said that nothing is more self-

PART 3: REFLECTIONS

defeating than over-confidence. (I would learn the truth of this expression on that Friday). As I placed my right arm on the table—bending it to a ninety-degree angle and opening my palm to receive Eunice's hand—I was surprised to find Eunice putting her left arm on the table in a similar posture to my right arm. I thought to myself, "Not only am I wrestling a girl but also a lefty. Oh well, it'll be over quickly." Eunice's left hand fit snugly into my right hand and at the count of three, we began.

At first our arms were rigidly erect, with each person measuring the others strength. I decided to add a brief feint to allow Eunice to attack first, just to see what she was made of. Eunice pushed back strongly. I allowed my arm to tilt slightly toward the desk before correcting its descent. I then applied maximum pressure in a quick counter attack, designed to catch her by surprise and put her on defense. With this maneuver, my arm recovered to its original position and I immediately went in for the kill, pushing confidently with everything I had to force Eunice's arm to the table. Unfortunately, I was in for a big surprise.

Midway to the table, Eunice's arm became immovable, despite the amount of force I applied. Her arm was frozen solid as if secured inside of a block of cement. I knew then that I was in deep trouble. Slowly but relentlessly,

PART 3: REFLECTIONS

Eunice pushed my arm up and back to its previous downward descent. This time there was no stopping my fall. The contest over.

"Boy, that was tough," Eunice commented as we shook hands.

"I thought you had me for a while."

"I really misjudged you," I replied, congratulating Eunice on her leverage and timing.

"We'll have to do it again."

And we did, with me winning some matches and Eunice winning more than her share. Publicly, I attributed her success to her leverage and timing. But privately, I knew it was due to her consistency and superior arm strength.

By the time we both were in high school, Eunice had lost interest in arm wrestling and seldom competed—losing more often than she won and turning down many challenges. But I learned an important lesson from our ninth-grade contests. That is, while it is undoubtedly true that most males are physically stronger than most females, it is equally true that some females are stronger than some males. Eunice was proof of it.

I eventually lost contact with Eunice following high school graduation; and to this day do not know if she is even still alive. The last word I heard about her was from a

PART 3: REFLECTIONS

classmate who attended a class reunion some fifty years ago. He told me that Eunice had attended a cosmetology school after graduating, married a coal mining foreman, became a mother of five children and was operating her own hair salon. The super girl had become a super woman. Boy, did I ever misjudge Eunice.

PART 3: REFLECTIONS

Reunion

The yacht pulled slowly into the slip reserved for it in Sheepshead Bay, Long Island. Patricia was holding onto the dock eagerly waiting for one of its passengers to disembark. She was excited about meeting the passenger since the two of them had not seen each other for more than 20 years.

Identical twins, Patricia and her sister, Rosalind, had been separated at the age of four, after the deaths of their parents in a horrific two-car accident on the Long Island Freeway. Both parents had a sole sister as their descendent. The two surviving sisters, Emma and Beatrice, could not agree on who would assume responsibility for the two nieces. So, they compromised with each aunt agreeing to take one girl and raise her separately from the other. Everyone involved agreed that it was a bad idea and not necessarily good for the girls; but it was the only practical solution the two aunts could agree on. Emma and Beatrice promised that the two girls would periodically be in touch with each other but over the ensuing years that promise was not kept.

Emma, the maternal aunt who assumed custody of Patricia, resided in Long Island—the home of her deceased

PART 3: REFLECTIONS

sister and brother-in-law prior to their deaths. Beatrice, the paternal aunt who assumed custody of Rosalind, flew back to her home in California with Rosalind after the funeral. A number of arguments occurred between the two aunts, the nature of which was a mystery to Patricia. The phone service was disconnected, and any letters sent to Aunt Beatrice's last known address were returned undelivered. Subsequently, the phone calls between the two girls dwindled until there was no contact between them at all.

Patricia was eight years old at the time. The only thing she recalled was that the two aunts had stopped speaking to each other. Aunt Emma insisted that it was due to her father's sister, Beatrice, wanted nothing to do with the rest of the family, speculating that she had married someone wealthy who could afford her luxurious lifestyle and the international travel Beatrice desperately craved for. Patricia never fully accepted her Aunt's speculative comments but, with the passage of time, found that the memory and yearning for her sister was slowly fading way.

Patricia was 24 years old when her Aunt Emma died. By then, she was a college graduate and immensely enjoying her first career as a Public Relations Specialist, for one of the country's leading advertising agencies. Upon arriving home

PART 3: REFLECTIONS

one evening, she was shaken to her core after listening to a recorded message on her phone:

"Hi, Patricia. If this is the right Patricia, I'm your twin sister, Rosalind. Aunt Beatrice died last year, leaving me owner of the yacht originally owned by her late husband. I'm married now and my husband and I are on a journey to revisit and reclaim my past. We do a lot of sailing. Our yacht is scheduled to dock at Slip 22 in Sheepshead Bay, Long Island on the 30th of October around 12 noon. I hope we can meet. We have a lot of catching up to do. I love you, Patricia."

Patricia paused for minute reminiscing over all the lost time and everything they had gone through. "I love you too, Rosalind," she whispered.

PART 3: REFLECTIONS

Sam Adams, Jr.

As far back as he could remember, Sam Adams, Jr. loved football. His passion for the game was inspired by the daily stories his mother would share concerning his dad's amazing achievements on the football field. The senior Adams was a star running back on the high school football team. He had done two things in rapid-fire order after his graduation: One, he married Sam, Jr.'s mother, Gracie; and two, he joined the United States Marines. A month prior to Sam, Jr's. birth, his father was killed in the line of duty.

Sam, Jr. could not pinpoint the exact moment when he decided to become a football star like his dad. Maybe it was when he caught his first football when he was only three years old. Then again, maybe it was due to the promise he showed in sports after his mother let him join the midget league football team.

Sam, Jr. excelled on the midget league football team and was easily counted as the best player in the league. Despite his rather small physique he could do it all—throw, catch and run—with his forte being speed and elusiveness. However, his aspirations to play varsity football in high school hit a snag when he was told he would have to bulk up more. Both his mother and coaches were hoping that he

PART 3: REFLECTIONS

would experience a growth spurt once he entered into his teen years. They knew that the players Sam, Jr. would be forced to compete against, would eventually become bigger and stronger as they got older. In order for Sam to compete, he would need to grow taller and bulk up his slimmer frame. Unfortunately, it never happened. This is when Sam, Jr. began to hear from detractors and doubters:

"You're too small to play varsity football!"

"Your body can't take the kind of hits some of these big guys can deliver!"

"You'll never play like your dad," they said.

Sam took it all in but said nothing. He was determined to prove them all wrong. The average player was around 5'10" and weighing 180 lbs. compared to Sam, Jr's 5'8" stature and 150 lbs. Nevertheless, Sam, Jr. was undaunted in his desire to play varsity football.

"I can't make myself taller. But with exercise, diet and weight lifting I can make my body as hard, muscular and compact as possible, without losing any speed or agility," he thought to himself.

Sam made a point of working out every day during recess, prior to when the varsity football season began. When the regular season practice started, he was among the first players on the field. The high school record for football

PART 3: REFLECTIONS

achievements now bears the names of two Adams—Sam Adams, Sr. and Sam Adams, Jr. No one could be prouder of Sam, Jr. than his mom.

PART 3: REFLECTIONS

Echo the Houseguest

"What an unusual name I said to my daughter, as she introduced me to her new puppy, Echo (pronounced "eck-o"). Echo was a small French-bred Papillion with a heavy white coat and brown ears. A handsome and intelligent dog—perky, friendly and frisky, all at the same time. One weekend while puppy sitting, with him as my sole house guest, I found out that he was also a perpetually demanding dog, given to prolonged periods of incessant barking when he does not get his way.

Being the old curmudgeon that I am, I made certain that he did not always get his way. The problem, I finally figured out, was that Echo thought he was a human. Although a dog himself, he could have cared less about other dogs. His barking did not come from an urge to be protective or belligerent, but rather it was his way of having a conversation. By the end of his stay with me, I had learned to keep him under control by periodically exchanging a few barks with him. The conversation would end when one or both of us felt a sense of hoarseness coming on.

Echo finally went home with my daughter. While I am enjoying the perpetual peace and quiet, I sort of miss our barking times together.

PART 3: REFLECTIONS

The Matador and The Bull

Boxing is not everyone's cup of tea. But the sport, in its basic brutality, can at times be a work of art. Especially, when two fighters of equal talent and different fighting styles meet in the ring. Such was the case of the story regarding the Matador and the Bull:

The fighter slowly circled around the ring, stalking his elusive opponent and trying to trap him in a corner. It was a vivid clash of styles between a boxer and a slugger. Joe Thunder (the "Bull") had been fighting professionally for only a year and a half, but he had already chalked up six impressive victories, knocking out his opponents in three rounds or less.

Joe's opponent (the "matador") was vastly different. He had won all of his fights too but only after out boxing his opponents. As the two entered into round four of the match, Joe noted that this opponent was not staying in one place long enough for Joe to hit him with one of his powerful punches. The matador continuously bobbed and weaved, dipped his shoulders and stayed on his toes, easily avoiding Joe's bull-like rushes to pin him down to any one section of the ring.

PART 3: REFLECTIONS

"Boy, this guy is cute," Joe thought to himself, as they began round five.

"Sooner or later, he's going to run out of gas and he'll be all mine. All it will take is one solid blow and he will cave like the rest of them," Joe murmured.

Round six came and Joe's opponent was far from caving in. Instead, to everyone's surprise, he was beginning to take the fight to Joe while avoiding Joe's clumsy and telegraphed counter punches. Having a much faster hand speed, Joe's opponent came at him with a frontal attack—punching Joe from angles, peppering Joe's face with jabs and occasionally taking round house swings at his torso, then gleefully dancing away before Joe could return fire.

Joe was a tough guy but he was beginning to feel the cumulative effect of all the blows and was slowly tiring. He was not used to going so many rounds with an opponent. Even though he was beginning to hurt, he remained confident that he would eventually prevail. Joe's manager, on the other hand, was not that certain. During the scheduled break after round six, his manager said:

"Joe, you've got to knock this guy out. You can't win on points."

"I ain't never had to win on no points and I don't plan to start now," Joe blurted.

PART 3: REFLECTIONS

"I knock people out. This guy can't run forever. I'm going to get him this round."

The manager smiled admiringly at Joe for his bravado, but he knew it would take a lucky punch for Joe to prevail over this obviously skilled fighter. As the bell rang for round seven Joe rushed across the ring determined to get within punching distance of his opponent. He paid for this recklessness as a steady rhythm of stinging jabs from his stealth-like foe tattooed his face. Although Joe was eating rubber, he kept coming, swinging wildly and proclaiming:

"I'm a bull and I'm going to crush you," he said.

The other fighter just smiled, which infuriated Joe even more. He took another wild swing and lost his balance, almost slipping on the canvas and exposing his full facial countenance to his opponent. This time the blows over each of his eyes felt different, as if his skin was ripping apart. His sight was quickly becoming blurred:

"I can't see," Joe screamed, as the referee separated the two fighters.

The referee took a quick look at the deep cuts on both eyebrows. A scarlet liquid of blood was flowing copiously down Joe's eyelids and into his eyes—eventually dripping onto his gloves and trunks, and finally resting in a pool on the canvas floor. The referee had an easy decision to make.

PART 3: REFLECTIONS

He had to stop the fight. Slowly and reluctantly, he lifted the arm of Joe's opponent in victory. In the same motion he looked at Joe with a nod of appreciation for his gallantry.

The Bull had been gallant but the Matador had won.

PART 3: REFLECTIONS

Confessions of an Unusual Dog

To understand this story, you are required to do two things: One, suspend your natural human arrogance; and two, expand your imagination. Come journey with me into the twilight zone:

Ok, I get it. I'm a dog.

I have four legs and large floppy ears.

I have a small body covered by thick white hair and brown splotches.

I have a medium length tail that constantly wiggles to denote what mood I'm in.

My nose, mouth and paws define me as a dog.

So, I accept my place in the animal kingdom.

Question is, why am I more at home with humans than dogs?

I hate doggy parks with all that running, barking, yipping and yapping.

On the rare occasions I agree to go, I snuggle close to my human family as possible while they entice me to socialize.

"Get away mutts!" I utter more than once.

I turned up my tail and walk away from their unwelcome intrusion into my space.

PART 3: REFLECTIONS

Maybe I'm just uppity—just an uppity Papillion.

That's my breed, you know.

I don't see too many of us in the parks these days.

But when I do, I don't socialize with them either.

You see, I'm different from them too.

I'm a dog who knows how humans think.

I recognize their speech regardless of what language they speak.

Of course, I don't let on that I know what they are saying and for one good reason:

It might frighten them and then they might label me as a freak.

I wouldn't like that very much because, well you see, I've grown accustomed to the free room and board.

To spur conversation between us, I have learned to adjust my barks to imitate the sounds of their speech.

But despite my best efforts, they can't differentiate from one bark to another.

In all honesty, sometimes it's frustrating being a dog with a Ph.D—a potential Rhodes Scholar—having to deal with owners who feel my vocabulary is limited to such basic words as "come here, sit up, lay down, stay, good boy, fetch and catch!"

PART 3: REFLECTIONS

I thought I had adjusted to their self-imposed limitations on my capabilities, until one day I heard my clueless owners speaking about getting me a four-legged companion.

Not a dog of my size or a cat but the odd companionship of a German Shepherd.

My initial instinctive thought was to resist the transaction.

But then I thought, "Why not?"

For this time only, I'll overcome my anti-dog attitude and teach him everything I know about humans. We can turn this companionship experience into real fun."

I can visualize it all now.

After the mandatory sniffing each other out, I bark, "Arf, arf!"

And the German Shepherd will respond, "Wolf, wolf!"

In dog translation, I am telling my shepherd friend, "These humans are strange."

In response he replies, "Let's humor them!"

Humans are so predictable.

After observing what good companions we made, they simply smile, offer a few simple commands and toss us a treat.

PART 3: REFLECTIONS

My shepherd friend and I smile at each other, waiting in anticipation before lunging for our treats.

I must make it a priority to school my new shepherd friend on everything I know about human speech.

After a while, it will be just another day in the life of two extraordinary dogs.

These humans have no idea that we know more than what they do.

But promise not to tell anyone because it is a dog's secret!

PART 3: REFLECTIONS

The Vote

It was November 1, 1959. Sam Brown, a 64-year-old cotton farmer from the southern region of Alabama, called the *Black Belt,* on this particular day was a very happy man. The mail box had just presented him with the prized possession of his life: A state issued voter registration card.

"Hallelujah," he shouted in unmitigated joy.

"I can finally vote!"

A life-long bachelor, Sam was born on November 1, 1895. He still lived at the site of his birth, even though the original plantation cabin where his parents once lived and called home had long since been renovated.

John and Eula Mae Brown loved their only child. But they could only express that love in their hearts and not in material things. They were tenant farmers and sharecroppers. They had worked the same cotton fields their parents had worked and toiled before them as slaves. None of them had ever voted or even thought of voting because their focus was on sheer day-to-day survival.

But Sam was different. Although he had only completed the third grade, before joining his parents in the fields fulltime, he made up for his lack of formal education by reading every history and social science book he could

PART 3: REFLECTIONS

get his hands on. He understood the plight of his family's deprivations and thought their needs would be better served if Blacks in the heavily populated Black Belt began to register and vote.

The White ruling class understood this too and constantly created barriers to prevent or slow down Black voter registration. These barriers took on the form of anything from poll taxes, arbitrary verbal and written quizzes on Alabama's State constitution to veiled and not so veiled physical threats by Klan riders. The goal was to intimidate potential voters to maintain their control. These intimidation tactics largely worked. As a result, only a small minority of the Black population registered and voted. Sam's parents were not among those who did.

When Sam was 18 he joined the U.S. Army to fight in World War I. Now, some forty years after discharge and after the deaths of his parents who never voted, Sam Brown was getting ready to vote.

He held the voter registration card in his hands and looking up to the heavens said simply, "mom and dad, we did it. I'll be voting for you too."

PART 3: REFLECTIONS

To Believe or Not Believe

I do not believe in horoscopes, especially those directed towards me while watching a television show. After a good night's sleep, I would get up the next morning and go ahead with life as usual.

The only difference is I would throw salt gently over my left shoulder and hot bacon grease at the screen door for good luck as I left for work.

On my way to work, I might make a slight deviation in my usual driving routine like taking a different route.

As I parked my car to walk the short distance to my office, I would be on the lookout for any black cat that might cross my path or any ladders least I unknowingly find myself walking underneath them. Yep, despite any doomsday horoscope prediction, I would otherwise have a normal day.

I must confess—in my final analysis—maybe I am bit more agnostic about horoscopes than I am an atheist.

PART 3: REFLECTIONS

The Seasons

WINTER. Picturesque mountains, of varying heights from the Allegheny mountain chain, surround a cluster of yellow and brown cookie cutter bungalows anchored on cinder blocks and concrete slabs in the scenic mining villages surrounding Bramwell, West Virginia. The homes and stores in the communities were largely built by the mining companies, the region's largest employer.

A small creek runs along the mountains' edge connecting Bramwell-home of millionares-to the various communities along with winding mountain roads. Driving over, around and through the mountains by tunnel, heading down towards the valley, one can see Bramwell and clusters of similar villages separated by small forests. It is winter time. The first heavy snow has arrived, filling the villages of the valley with a seamless white blanket of snow that projects a picture of peace, tranquility and harmony with nature. The leaves of the evergreen trees are laden with snow and chimneys from bungalow fireplaces are belching trails of black smoke that dissipate into the chilly, pristine air. One hesitates to disturb the snow with a footprint.

SPRING. The village of Bramwell awakens from its winter slumber and the formerly barren trees on the

PART 3: REFLECTIONS

surrounding mountains fill their branches with nutrients that give life to leaves. Soon the mountains are awash with mushrooming colors of varying shades of green. In the valleys blades of green grass engage in mortal combat with colorful, sturdy weeds intent on receiving landscape dominance. The air, although still brisk, has now lost some of its winter chill.

SUMMER. The warm air from the rays of the summer sun sweeps through the villages of the valley. The yards around the unfenced cottages blend into a sea of green. The mountain trees are full of leaves. The night brings a cool breeze. At the height of Summer and on the warmest days, bungalow porches are the most popular places to be as windows are opened to circulate the air and bring relief from the stifling heat.

FALL. As leaves go through their end of life cycle, slowly dying before falling to the ground, they unleash a rainbow of colors. Fall has begun. The air slowly loses its summer warmth. Ever changing colors in and around the villages are a barometer for the onset of winter. The cycle repeats itself. Despite the weather changes, villages remain the same.

PART 3:

REFLECTIONS

PART 3: REFLECTIONS

EDGAR and La VERNE RUSSELL

PART 3: REFLECTIONS

EDGAR and La VERNE RUSSELL WEDDING

PART 3: REFLECTIONS

EDGAR RUSSELL, JR.

PART 3: REFLECTIONS

MOM & DAD

AUTHOR (holding picture of wife) & ADULT CHILDREN

FAMILY

PART 3: REFLECTIONS

DAUGHTER'S WEDDING

PART 3: REFLECTIONS

AUTHOR'S MOTHER

GRAND-DAUGHTER

DAUGHTER & GRAND-DAUGHTER

PART 3: REFLECTIONS

THE LEGACY OF LOVE FOR...58 YEARS!

Memoirs
and
MISCELLANEOUS Ramblings

www.ingramcontent.com/pod-product-compliance
Lightning Source LLC
Chambersburg PA
CBHW071855110526
44591CB00011B/1416